THE ANGEL WORKBOOK

THE ANGEL WORKBOOK

A PRACTICAL GUIDE TO INTERPRETING DIVINE MESSAGES

✦ A N N I E   B U R D I C K ✦

ULYSSES PRESS

Published by:
Ulysses Press
P.O. Box 3440
Berkeley, CA 94703
www.ulyssespress.com

ISBN: 978-1-64604-416-0
Library of Congress Catalog Number: 2022936259

Printed in the United States by Versa Press
10 9 8 7 6 5 4 3 2 1

Acquisitions editor: Claire Sielaff
Managing editor: Claire Chun
Editor: Cathy Cambron
Proofreader: Beret Olsen
Front cover design: Thanh Ly
Interior design and layout: Winnie Liu
Cover art: © Evgeny Karandaev/shutterstock.com
Interior art: from shutterstock.com—header icons © Valedi; chapter clouds © Viky Y.ai; yoga
    poses © Babkina Svetlana; chakra chart © moibalkon

IMPORTANT NOTE TO READERS: This book has been written and published for informational and educational purposes only. It is not intended to serve as medical advice or to be any form of medical treatment. You should always consult with your physician before altering or changing any aspect of your medical treatment. Do not stop or change any prescription medications without the guidance and advice of your physician. Any use of the information in this book is made on the reader's good judgment and is the reader's sole responsibility. This book is not intended to diagnose or treat any medical condition and is not a substitute for a physician. This book is independently authored and published, and no sponsorship or endorsement of this book by, and no affiliation with, any trademarked brands or other products mentioned within is claimed or suggested. All trademarks that appear in this book belong to their respective owners and are used here for informational purposes only. The author and publisher encourage readers to patronize the brands mentioned in this book.

For my Aunt Wendy,
the best and cutest girl in the world—
and someone I'd consider an angel on earth.

CONTENTS

INTRODUCTION

It is life's nature to challenge us. Living on earth means accepting the messy, wildly complex, never stagnant nature of things—some days reveling in beauty and joyous fortune, other days blanketed by the weight of challenges or grief. We've been told—and perhaps even understand consciously—that it's impossible to fully understand and appreciate the great and wonderful parts of life without experiencing the hard days and crushing sadness that can come, too. We feel love and joy more freely because we also know their darker, steelier opposites.

Even so, when those difficult moments inevitably arrive, when negative emotions take over the subconscious, we naturally seek solutions, guidance, even tangible support. Unpayable bills, medical challenges, heartbreak, strained family relationships, ailing loved ones, accidents, global crises—these things feel insurmountable at times. Our bodies and minds hold up when they can, and at other times, they threaten to break under the weight of hurt and fear.

In such moments, many of us turn to spiritual wisdom. Whether or not we're religious, we think *maybe* there is some force or being or power out there that can guide, nurture, and take the bad feelings away, at least for a moment. And whether or not we do any-thing to find that guidance, whether we ever actually form a connection, we're not wrong in thinking there's something out there. There's plenty out there, in fact. We just have to know how to see the connections and how to create them ourselves.

Communicating and forming loving relationships with angels may seem like a foreign concept to you. Or it may feel totally familiar. In large part, how you feel may depend on your spiritual upbringing and perspectives on spirituality and the divine at this point in your life. If you're open to all possibilities of the universe, and perhaps already exploring some of the more "unexplainable" aspects of spirituality and life (whether that's developing psychic ability, using divination tools, trying alternative healing therapies, diving into spell work, or something else altogether), adding angelic communication into the mix probably doesn't feel like a huge stretch. Likewise, if your childhood or adult life includes religious practices that incorporate angels and divine communication, again, you probably don't see building your own angel network as all that odd.

But even if this world is totally new to you—if perhaps you're simply looking for an explanation for a miracle or a new way to ground yourself in the universe—you're still in the right place.

This book aims to guide and inform without ever forcing your perspective on angels and any relationships you build with them to look a particular way. There is no one way to approach divine communication, but there are myriad ways to dive into your spiritual world and reap incredible benefits for your mental wellness, health, relationships, and anything else you desire.

The emphasis here is on practice more than intensive study. While still providing all the essential basics and background information on various elements of angel work and communication—from interpreting angel numbers to journaling and connecting—you'll find more hands-on tools than endless pages of history and theory. After all, working with angels is a practice, not just a concept. If you truly want to make it a part of your life, understanding the essential tenets and then putting them to work is the best method. Each chapter includes a range of real-world tools, from journaling pages to exercises, meditations, and collaborative journeys. This is your space now, where you can scribble, write, reflect, cross things out, and try them again. These pages are sacred, not in a way that prohibits interaction and getting them messy, but in a way that invites that response. This workbook is your space, so make the most of it.

Tackling some—or best, all—of the exercises laid out here will guide you on your journey to a life filled with angelic communication, deep love, and spiritual guidance whenever you need it. The angels can't wait to be a part of your life. All you need to do now is step forward, take a deep breath, and dive in.

CHAPTER 1

HOW WE THINK ABOUT ANGELS: NEW PERSPECTIVES

For many of us, of course depending on our upbringing, the instinct when thinking of angels is to ascribe to them a religious association. And in fairness, this is a traditional and comfortable approach that many angel communicators use to this day. They practice religion and find that the angel stories of that theology resonate strongly with them. This is wonderful and a great option—but not the only option. In recent decades, a new wave (though I'm sure you've heard it described as a "New Age," right?) of spiritually minded but nonreligious individuals have found new ways to appreciate angelic guidance outside the confines of structured religion. Some also opt for other methods of connecting to the wisdom of the earth, nature, and spirit, whether through the use of crystals, meditation, runes, psychic exploration, spell work, or something else altogether. Many people use a range of methods in their preferred and most comfortable ways, all with the purpose of feeling more connected to energy, Source, the space they inhabit, and the people around them.

At the end of the day, we're all seeking clarity, peace, and a fulfilling life. The methods you use to get there, as long as they're founded in positivity and do no harm, are all valid and wonderful ways to work toward your self-growth and greatest potential.

Before you spend a whole book learning how to connect with angels, understand their messages, and improve your life, it's still important to get that essential background information. But while there are dozens of incredible books out there that specifically dig into the history and stories of angels (and you should explore those if that topic interests you!), this book is first and foremost meant to be *practical*, a workbook to lead you through real-life practices and methods for embracing angels. The history and background in this book are kept simple so as not to overwhelm you while preparing you for your future communications.

A BRIEF HISTORY OF ANGELS

To call any history of angels brief is a bit of false advertising, since in actuality, their written history spans thousands of years and numerous texts and theologies. Depictions and mentions of angels show up in Sumerian stone carvings, the founding of Zoroastrianism, and ancient Mesopotamia.[1] Later, angels would be adopted into Judaism, then Christianity, and later Islam as well. Even Hinduism and Buddhism, while not celebrating or referring to angels specifically as those other religions do, still have spiritual guides and figures who play extremely similar roles.

In the Christian context, which is perhaps the one in which angels are most at the forefront in a modern American setting, we often picture the celebration of Christmas, a tradition that has angels—winged, lighting the sky, and often topping trees—at its very heart. But even in Christianity, the depiction of angels has steadily evolved over time. The Bible clearly mentions angels as messengers of God but provides minimal detail, leaving religious interpreters to wonder and speculate about the appearance and purpose of angels for centuries.

So, from the early centuries of the church, there has been much discussion about whom angels served on the earthly plane and what form they would take when providing

---

1   Richard Webster, *Angels for Beginners* (Woodbury, MN: Llewellyn Worldwide, 2017), 12–13.

their wisdom. According to an article that appeared in *National Geographic*, "at early Christian monasteries, for instance, many ascetics assumed that really good students would get some kind of divine guide or coach to help them." The writer adds, "in the towns, though, a more democratic view of angels prevailed. Bishops and other officials began to assure their congregants that everyone has a guardian angel."[2] This "democratic" view is the one taken by most of those who seek angelic guidance and look for their communications nowadays. And it's true: You don't have to be "blessed" in some way, belong to a particular religion (or any), or live a certain life to have angels in your corner, looking out and intervening if needed. They're just there, and the big step for most of us is learning to interpret messages and communicate in return.

Judaism, like Christianity, includes a strong belief in angels. However, their presentation and purpose are different. While Christians tend to celebrate angels and even worship them as divine, godly, and key players in stories such as the birth of Jesus, the Jewish faith takes a different perspective. In this religious context, angels are messengers and worshippers of God only. And, notes Richard Webster, "unlike the Christian tradition, Jewish angels are programmed to do specific tasks. Some angels are created to perform one particular task, and, once this task has been accomplished, the angel ceases to exist."[3] Obviously, this is a major departure from the Christian interpretation and from the one most New Age angel practitioners and communicators follow. If, however, this perspective aligns with your religious beliefs, it's also a perfectly valid way to view angels and their purpose. Ultimately, whatever your background and belief system tells you about angels, you can choose how you'll see them and interact with them in your life and go on from there.

---

2   Brian Handwerk, "Evolution of Angels: From Disembodied Minds to Winged Guardians," *National Geographic*, December 24, 2011.
3   Webster, *Angels for Beginners*, 16–17.

ANGELIC HIERARCHY

Now, with a very synopsized version of angelic history in mind, there's also a lot to gain in a basic understanding of the traditional hierarchy of angels, which you may or may not choose to incorporate into your practice.

Early Christian writers were the ones to create this hierarchy, outlining the ranks and positions of various angels in their support of God. While this hierarchy is important in Christian and Jewish faiths, it doesn't appear in any others, so you can choose how much stock you place in it. That being said, the centuries of strong belief in this hierarchy have certainly enforced its potential power, and using it as an outline, especially when you are a beginner to angel communication, can absolutely help ground your practice and allow you to follow along with some of the key players. However, if you're someone who feels more free-spirited about divine guidance and would prefer not to contact a particular angel or follow a hierarchy, that's more than OK, too!

SIMPLIFIED ANGELIC HIERARCHY

Again, books can be and have been filled simply with outlines of the religious backgrounds of angels and their complex hierarchical system. However, since this system is so complicated and exists only in a few religions, for our practical purposes a much pared-down version is a great starting point. If you feel drawn to angelic hierarchy or particular levels, try continuing your research by exploring some of the texts and articles that dive into this topic in particular.

Let's start with the hierarchical levels. These begin with the angels closest to God and move down from there in angels' importance and ability.

TRIAD 1	TRIAD 2	TRIAD 3
1. Seraphim	1. Dominions/Dominations	1. Principalities
2. Cherubim	2. Virtues	2. Archangels
3. Thrones	3. Power	3. Angels

Some of this information may surprise you. Richard Webster sums the situation up perfectly in *Angels for Beginners*: "If the seraphim are generals, the angels are privates in God's army. The members of this group are the angels most likely to be seen by humans. There are millions of angels in this group, and although they have been frequently seen by people, they are not usually identified by name."[4] Knowing about the existence of high-ranking groups is interesting and can inform your communications, but keep in mind that we humans who seek angelic communications are usually talking to angels in this lowest (though still enormously important) tier, and occasionally to an archangel, perhaps in the form of a meditation.

Now, let's cover a few key players among the archangels. You may have heard some of these names before. You may also find you connect to one of them in particular and may wish to direct some of your letters, journals, or meditations toward them.

Michael: The best known of the group, he is seen as a protector figure in the Catholic Church. He's also considered to be closest to God of any archangel. He represents love and serves as a warrior and compassionate guide.

Gabriel: With a name that is also well known among Christians, Gabriel is considered a prophet and is often depicted as female, though angels are typically considered not to have gender. Typically, Gabriel is associated with overcoming things such as sensitivity and fear.

Uriel: Said to "meet the souls of sinners as they arrive in heaven," Uriel is associated often with music and with repentance.[5]

Raphael: Another high-ranking archangel, Raphael is considered a guide for healing, both emotional and physical.

---

4   Webster, *Angels for Beginners*, 34–35.
5   Richard Webster, *Spirit Guides and Angel Guardians* (Woodbury, MN: Llewellyn Worldwide, 1998), 21.

Other archangels you may hear about as you dig into angelic communication include Ariel, Chamuel, Raguel, and Jeremiel. However, remember that while you may call on a specific archangel for wisdom on a topic the archangel is associated with, often the angels who come to support us are lower-ranking and unnamed and will be the ones meant specifically for you.

PURPOSEFUL EXERCISE

Begin Your Angel Journal

While some of the prompts and exercises in this book will provide lined space to jot your thoughts and replies, this is also the time to begin your own, dedicated journal for the purpose of reflecting on and recording your angel communications. This is simple! Follow these quick steps, and you'll be ready to dive into the exercises to come.

1. Head to your room, office, or the store to hunt for the perfect notebook. If you're like me, you may already have a stack of blank notebooks collected over the years. Here's your perfect chance to put one to use. If not, purchase a blank journal that calls to you. Make sure you're drawn to the design, and choose lined or unlined paper based on your own taste.

2. Decorate the cover so you know exactly what the book is for and so you feel motivated to pick it up. The more visually appealing (and harder to lose) the journal is, the better.

3. Bring your blank book with you to a quiet, peaceful space. Do a full meditation if you're so inclined, but at the very least, put a hand on the book, close your eyes, and repeat this or something similar:

> Angels and guides, creating this journal marks my first step in communicating with you and seeking to make you a part of my life. I am channeling my energy, positivity, and love into everything I do with this journal. Please reach out in any way, and know that I'm learning to notice and absorb your messages.

JOURNALING EXERCISE

What Angels Mean to You

Having started exploring the background of angels in this chapter (and perhaps in other reading you've taken on), it's a great time to break in your angel journal by writing down some of your personal experiences, thoughts, and opinions on angels. Not only is this a great way to prepare yourself for future steps such as communication, but it also will be helpful for you to look back on once you're more established in your practice, so you can see whether your views of angels have evolved or changed at all over time.

In your journal, write anything that comes to mind with the following questions. And remember, you don't need to filter yourself—this journal is private, just for you and your growth.

✦ Before ever reaching out to them, what are your thoughts about angels? Do you have a religious background or history that frames the way you view angels?

✦ Have you ever had an experience that might have involved communication from angels? (You might not be sure right now; we'll touch more on ways angels reach out in future sections!)

✦ Reading the basic overviews, do you feel pulled toward any archangel in particular? (You might not, and that's just fine!)

✦ What might you like to seek support or guidance on?

CHAPTER 2

CONNECTING WITH ANGELS AND THE DIVINE

Having a foundational understanding of angels and divine guardians is the first and most obvious key to being able to connect with them and use their presence to enrich your life. But going forward from there is likely the most daunting part of this journey. Believing in the existence or power of divine spirits is one thing, but doing the internal and external work to make them part of your life is another. This work can take time and patience.

Rest assured, even if the process feels like a challenge, angels will be excited to connect with you and will often meet you halfway once you start the process of engaging and connecting. They want to be a part of your life.

There are a number of ways that you might ultimately connect with angels or any divine presence, including angel journaling, which will be covered thoroughly in chapter 5. Here are a few other methods to keep in mind.

UNINTENTIONAL CONNECTION

Yep, many people find themselves getting in touch with angels, or experiencing their messages or interventions, without doing anything to seek them out. These connections will likely be totally unexpected, and you actually may have come across these moments in your life already, with or without understanding their significance. Whether they have taken the form of meaningful symbols, such as white feathers or shimmering, sparkling lights; a voice in your head leading and guiding you; a seemingly miraculous event or moment; or a full, embodied angelic vision, angels may have already been playing a role in your life, behind the scenes. Now you'll be able to spot these instances and interpret them more easily.

MEDITATING INTO AWARENESS

While not a traditional meditation style, this method is still essentially like other forms of meditation: calming your mind and body, readying yourself to accept wisdom, and then calling for it to come to you. You can tailor this process to yourself and the ways you most innately relax and connect to spiritual guidance, but at its core, this is a process of finding quiet, private space; sinking into a peaceful state; and then calling to angels and waiting for a response to come. This process may not work on the first try, or even on the fifth. But over time, calming your mind and making it a more aware and accepting place will eventually bring you to a space where you can engage with angels and receive their messages.

PAYING MORE ATTENTION

As with unintentional connections, this method may not involve explicitly saying, "Hello angels, please come give me wisdom!" Instead, this method likely involves more personal growth and development of your attention skills. Knowing everything you do about angelic connection—and armed with everything you'll learn in the coming chapters as well—you can start focusing in on some more subtle signs and messages that may have been popping up when your mind was too preoccupied to receive and understand them.

Have you ever started hearing unusual or repeating sounds, such as sporadic buzzing, humming, or bells? This may be attempted angel contact. (Persistent and nonstop sounds should be checked by a doctor, though! We're talking about occasional odd noises without a clear source.) The same goes for fleeting, beautiful scents or tastes in your mouth. A wafting floral scent or one that engages a beloved, core memory and seems to pop up out of nowhere can simply be a sign that an angel is around and nudging you. Pay attention, too, to flares of emotions that seem to arrive and dissipate without a clear reason. While we're all prone to emotional cycling and swings, an unexpected flood of intense love or joy unrelated to what's happening physically around you is a great indicator that something is going on behind the scenes. Odd physical sensations, such as a shiver or a brush of air on your neck, can also indicate a presence making contact.

Ultimately, being more mindful and aware of these potential signs and moments of engagement can get you started on a path to more regular angelic communication. Once you know some of the indicators that your guardian angel or spiritual guides are around, you'll be ready to recognize them and start communicating back.

WRITING LETTERS

If meditating or speaking aloud feels like more of a hurdle to you, writing down your thoughts and intended communications can be equally effective. However, this process should be a bit more specific. Rather than sitting down peacefully and saying, "I'm ready to communicate," you'll be putting thoughts to paper. That takes a bit more thought and intention, and preferably a specific recipient as well. Try to direct your letter to the one angel or presence you'd like to contact for help or connection, rather than a collective group. Then, write with a purpose. If you're connecting for the first time, introduce yourself. Your letter should aim to address a specific concern or question that's a focus in your life right now. Describe your feelings, worries, or thoughts in detail. Putting all of this on paper is honestly as good for your ability to handle the situation as it is for connecting you to some angelic guidance. Even if you're not talking about a life issue but perhaps are expressing your interest in forming a deeper connection with this particular angel, be specific and direct. Explain what you hope to gain from the communication and relationship, and specific questions you have for the angel. Consider including a request for how the angel may get in contact with you—for example, "If you're able to give signs of your presence through white feathers or floral scents, I'll know you're connecting with me." Be sure to include genuine words of thanks and appreciation for this angel's work and guidance in your life. And conclude with a loving signature. As with any letter, use an envelope, and add the angel's name to the front. If possible, take a meditative moment to "send" this letter off. Light a small candle, get quiet, and reflect on the things you've written and the recipient you have in mind. Giving your appreciation and love, carefully burn the letter in the candle's flame, releasing the message to the angel it's meant for.

JOURNALING EXERCISE

Readying for Connection

As you prepare yourself to try one or several methods for reaching angels and receiving divine guidance, it's a great idea to start with some reflective journaling and note-taking. This is the beginning of a wild and beautiful spiritual journey and path of growth. Having some thoughts recorded helps you not only to be more cognizant of your feelings and preparedness, but also to look back in the future at your mentality and perspectives during this time to see how they've changed.

Answer these questions on the lines provided, knowing the answers are only for yourself and your own process.

✦ What is your connection to angels and spirit now? What do you hope for it to look like in the future?

✦ Do you feel you've opened your heart and mind fully to the truth of angels? What more might you need to learn or do to fully accept this reality before trying to communicate?

✦ Do you have a specific intention in mind for your angelic communication, or do you hope to engage with one angel in particular?

Meditating to Connect

Let's dig a little deeper into the second method discussed earlier—meditating into awareness—and look at how this might go and how to try it for yourself. Some people have worked to become extremely practiced at meditation or inner reflection, while others have never tried it and may not even feel prepared to do so. Having a clear-cut, simple starting point makes meditation a lot less daunting. So here's one approach.

Start by finding a quiet space where you can have some time to yourself without interruptions. You may want to plan a time when others in your house will be gone or use a room that's personal to you. Wear something comfortable and choose a time when you're in a good headspace and feeling emotionally ready.

Avoid distractions. Ask the people in your home for some time, turn off your phone, close the door and perhaps the windows, and so on. Sit or lie down in a comfortable position.

Next, take time to relax your mind and body. Becoming relaxed can be easiest for different people in a variety of ways, depending on their unique needs and calm-down methods. As a baseline, try this intentional deep breathing set. Clearing your mind more with each cycle, start by breathing in deeply through your nose, for a count of four. Hold the breath for a count of four, then exhale the air through your mouth slowly and evenly, for another count of four. Do this cycle several times.

If deep breathing doesn't calm you enough, try a second step. Closing your eyes, picture a setting of pure bliss and relaxation. Picture, first, what you see around you in this setting, whether that's soothing waves, a verdant meadow, or some other dreamy oasis personal to you. Then, add the matching sounds of your peaceful scene. Next, picture vividly the scents encircling you in this place of tranquility. Imagine any feelings in your body or sensations on your skin—breeze, rain, sun, or anything else. Sit for as long as you feel called to in this richly imagined space of comfort and peace. When you do open your eyes and return to your reality, you should have a calmer, more open mindset.

Now, to reach out to angels: In this relaxed mindset, close your eyes again and set your intentions. Think clearly about your desires to connect with the angelic guides (perhaps using the answers you wrote out in the previous exercise). If it helps you, voice these desires aloud. Think specifically about the particular angel you may be looking to connect with, or think more generally about your guardian angel, if you prefer. Express your thanks for the angel's love and support in your life and your desire to connect and communicate with the angel on a more regular basis.

Then make a request. Ask something like, "Will communicating regularly be possible?" Then sit quietly and receptively, paying attention to any possible messages. A message may not be as direct as you expect—perhaps a small, clear voice in your head or a sensory shift. Most likely, you won't experience any connection at all on your first attempt. Don't stress. This is a slow, patient process, not something you can rush. The more times you repeat these steps, the clearer it will be to your guardian angel, or whomever you reach out to, that you're serious and dedicated to the idea of communicating.

Once you're able to establish communication, continue scaled-down versions of this process—or use your own method—to keep that line of communication open and clear so you can send or receive a message whenever you need to.

ACTIVE EXERCISE
Daydreaming with a Purpose

We have a tendency to put a lot more stock in the messages we receive during sleep and dreams than we might in the thoughts that come to us during daydreams. But why? Studies of people daydreaming have shown that, "when people's minds wandered in more fantastical ways (playing out implausible fantasies or bizarre, funny scenarios, for example) or in ways that seemed particularly meaningful to them, they tended to have more creative ideas and feel more inspired at the end of the day."[6] As it so happens, wild and free daydreaming (or meaningful daydreaming, which is essential here) can take you on the mental journeys needed to boost creativity and inspiration. The real key is to daydream the right way.

It's safe to say that there are better and worse moments to "mind-wander" or daydream. Drifting mentally off during important work, a conversation with a loved one, or a memorable event is going to vastly reduce your productivity or your memory of that situation. However, in a moment of calm and peace, with nothing more pressing for your attention to rest on, mind-wandering can be a huge boost to creativity, even helping you to reframe your ideas about a topic—or, perhaps, to receive angelic communication.

Try these steps for a slightly more intentional mind-wandering journey that could put you in contact with angelic wisdom.

1. Find time when you have nothing important to focus on and your mind can comfortably wander. In other words, this should not be a time when you should be working, caring for anyone, or getting to a commitment.

2. Choose a mundane or even mindless activity that you enjoy: knitting, doodling, washing dishes, folding clothes, shucking corn—you get the idea.

3. Settle in to start your activity, but consciously say to yourself, "It's OK for my mind to wander wherever it wants to. If angels see this time as an opportunity for connection, I welcome that."

4. Now, allow yourself to daydream as you normally would. Perhaps turn your wandering thoughts toward a part of your life you want guidance in, or just allow your mind to move naturally wherever it pleases.

---

6   Jill Suttie, "What Daydreaming Does to Your Mind," *Greater Good Magazine*, July 5, 2021, https://greatergood.berkeley.edu/article/item/what_daydreaming_does_to_your_mind.

5. Maintain a light awareness of which thoughts are your own and which may be messages from a guardian angel or other guide. Symbols, sounds, and voices may also appear and guide you.

6. When you've completed the activity or task you were doing or you need to carry on with your day, try to take a moment to jot down any thoughts you explored that surprised you or that seemed to be connected to a guide. Doing so will help you to uncover times when angels do get in touch, rather than letting communication slip by you unnoticed.

CHAPTER 3

HOW TO RAISE YOUR VIBRATION

If you've read any other book or article with New Age content, the idea of raising your vibration is probably nothing new. Frankly, it's the cornerstone and starting place for any more advanced pursuits, whether that's connecting to angels, goddesses, passed loved ones, and the like, or whether it's deepening your awareness, building a psychic connection, trying divination tools, or exploring anything else you might be curious about. Raising your vibration is an activity you can subtly and regularly infuse into your daily life through various methods and practices. The result will be a more open and accepting mind, ready to receive messages, spread joy, or get to a higher spiritual plane. Raising your vibration is also a key step in deepening your ability to connect with the angels and divine guides surrounding you.

But what is vibration raising all about? Well, our world is filled with vibrations. Each person or object you interact with is composed of countless molecules, all vibrating along with the earth we're on. Vibrations can be happening at different speeds or, in other words, can be higher or lower. If you enter a party or join a meeting and feel like you're reading the "vibes" in the room, you're already tuning into those vibrations, even if you're not doing so consciously. Chopra, a meditation-focused site and app, has a great way of describing vibrations: "A vibration is a state of being, the atmosphere, or the energetic quality of a person, place, thought, or thing." In other words, you can't see a vibration, but you can feel it—in the air around you, in the energy of a space, in the moods others around you are emanating, and so on.

As for raising your own vibrations, beyond making angel communication and psychic development easier, "higher vibes" will make you feel better, day in and day out. The ways to raise your vibration are essentially spiritual self-care practices—things you may already do. We've long been told meditation, deep breathing, and positive internal monologues make us happier—and they do! But why? A lot of the reason comes down to getting your vibration on a higher level, making you more energized, positive, and open to the experiences coming your way.

Here are a few vibration-raising practices you can incorporate into your weekly routine—if they're not already a part of it!

+ **Meditate:** Yep, no surprise here. Touted for its ample mental and physical health benefits, meditation is one of the best ways to raise those vibes to a high level and get you ready to send and receive messages to your guardian angel (or anyone, really!).

+ **Practice conscious gratitude:** Feelings of genuine gratitude for the people and blessings in your life have huge power. Spending some time each day reflecting on the things you're truly grateful for not only puts the hard stuff into perspective, but also will absolutely raise that vibration to the next level.

+ **Stretch and breathe:** Run through your favorite yoga routine. Or, if time doesn't allow, do five to ten minutes of your favorite moves or deep stretches. All the while, breathe deeply, intentionally, and rhythmically. Try to inhale for a set count (though the length is up to you), hold for the same count, and then exhale for another count.

+ **Try crystals:** Certainly more and more a mainstream thing, crystals are worth exploring. People who collect, display, and use crystals are often doing so (intentionally or not) for their vibration-raising abilities. Whether individuals want more clarity, positivity, energy, patience, or something else, they intentionally select crystals to keep in their home or on their person to get those vibrations flowing. If you've dismissed crystals so far, what have you got to lose by trying them out? They look lovely and just might make a difference as you follow your path to angel communication.

✦ **Be intentionally more positive:** Feeling down? Challenge yourself to release negative thoughts, even for a few moments, and focus on something good and joyful. Being around your pets can help, as can spending time with a friend or calling a loved one. Whenever possible, simply push positive energy into your mental space, even if it takes a bit of strain. Focus longer on the good thoughts and experiences than on the bad.

✦ **Give freely:** Generosity is absolutely a vibration raiser. Give when you're able and what you're able. If you don't have money to spare, this can simply mean cooking for loved ones or volunteering some time to help others. Perhaps you can clean out your closet and give clothes you never wear to someone who will value them. Maybe you can donate money to a cause or someone who's down on their luck. Or you may have something else to offer, such as mowing the lawn for your neighbor or babysitting for a friend. The more you can give of yourself and your abundance (while still giving yourself the things you need, too—don't forget about yourself!), the more you'll feel those positive effects on your vibration.

✦ **Detox:** I'm not talking fad dieting or drinking broth for every meal, but detoxifying your body of things such as alcohol, harmful substances, and even excess caffeine or sugar will help you feel more in tune with the positive energy of the world around you and keep your vibration less dimmed by toxins. These changes don't have to be permanent! Try taking a caffeine and alcohol break for a week and combine it with some meditation and see whether you feel a bit clearer and more in tune with your surroundings afterward.

✦ **Get outside:** Being around greenery and nature has been shown again and again in studies to be hugely beneficial to mental health, mood, and even body image. There's no question that those perks tie right in with raising your vibration. When you can, work outside, eat outside, take walks, go on hikes, and find time to be peaceful and enjoy the plants, trees, and fresh air around you.

Of course, this list of ways to raise your vibration is far from comprehensive. If these activities don't suit you, or you want more ways to raise those vibrations, just reflect on the self-care routines you already have or any habits you practice that help you feel immediately lighter, freer, and better afterward. Whether you recite mantras, journal, work out, eat natural foods, or prefer any other form of self-care, such practices are definitely part of your personal vibration-raising routine.

JOURNALING EXERCISE

What Raises Your Vibration?

Reflecting on all the potential ways to raise your vibration, both those just listed and those you've experienced in your own life, grab your angel journal and answer these questions about how you'll raise your vibration in the future.

✦ How do you feel about your vibration right now? Do you think you've been on a lower vibration or are you starting from a good place?

✦ What are the self-care routines you already have in your life? How do they help you?

✦ What practices might you try to add or incorporate into your routine to raise your vibration?

Practicing Gratitude

A hugely effective way to raise those vibrations is to be more actively grateful. Here are three potential ways to actively show and practice gratitude more in your everyday life. Try one or all of them and see how your emotions might change for the better.

1. Start journaling about gratitude. Whether in your angel journal or another daily journal, take a moment at the end of each day to jot down something that you felt deeply grateful for that day. Doing so might be more difficult on some days than others, but even noting "I was grateful for short lines at the grocery store" or "I appreciated getting a text from my friend" can remind you of the many things there are to be appreciative of, even on the hard days.

2. Say "thank you" more! Make a conscious effort to thank the people in your life for the kind things they do for you or even for the way they make you feel. Thank-yous don't have to be limited to times when someone hands you something. In fact, thanking a friend for being there for you in a hard moment, thanking your partner for doing a chore or planning a date, or thanking your parents for something you've always appreciated but never mentioned—these moments of gratitude will mean more for you and for them.

3. When you feel grateful, give back. This one is, in essence, an act of spreading kindness. If someone does something kind for you, something you feel grateful for, reflect on how you can take that positive feeling and share it with others. You might do the same thing for another person. For example, if you get a thoughtful text that makes you feel grateful for your friend, reach out to a friend you haven't communicated with in a while and share that positive feeling. Or simply channel those grateful feelings into something kind you can do for someone, whether a stranger or loved one.

4. Meditate on gratitude. If you like guided meditations, there are plenty of gratitude-focused options you can find with a quick search online. However, you can keep it simple, too. Take your favorite meditation position, breathe deeply, get into a restful headspace, and then recite some statements or mantras of gratitude. "I appreciate . . . today" or "I feel immense gratitude for my blessings and share them with the world" are great starting places.

Choosing Crystals to Deepen Your Practice

So, you're in the process of building connections with angels to improve your life and gain insights. If you don't already have some crystals to wear, hold during meditations, or put in meaningful locations around your home, it's a great time to get some! Crystals are excellent vibration raisers—and the individual properties of particular crystals can be even more advantageous to your spiritual practices and growth if you choose well. Keep in mind, though, no matter what the listed properties of a particular stone are, if you enter a shop with the stated intention of finding crystals to improve your angel connections and then feel very drawn to one stone in particular, that's likely a sign that it will be a great tool for you.

If you're new to crystals, heading to a shop in person, rather than shopping online, is a great option. Being there in person allows you the chance to talk to the experts working there, touch and feel various crystals, and really get a sense for the ones that call to you and may be best for your needs.

Before you go, set your intention. Speak aloud something like, "I'm going to look for crystals that will be valuable for enhancing my spiritual practice and make great tools for my angel communications. If I don't find anything today, that is OK, too. If any guides feel inclined to give me a sign that one crystal is best for me, I am open to receiving that message."

When you get to a shop, explore with an open mind and heart. Pay attention to any internal voices pointing you toward one stone or another. If something catches your eye again and again, that's another great sign. Ask questions and explore crystals you might not expect to like!

Of course, for many people, it helps to have some idea of crystal properties and what might make a great tool for a particular individual. Here are a few crystals you might seek out for their beneficial properties:

+ **Celestite:** a powerful enhancer of your divine intuition, and great for aiding in communication

+ **Seraphinite:** a very spiritually charged stone, perfect for connecting with angels and divine guides of all kinds

+ **Obsidian:** wards off negative energy and works to ground you in the space you occupy here in your life

+ **Citrine:** inspires creativity and motivation, helping you express yourself in powerful ways

+ **Angelite:** excellent for improving communication and the ability to speak freely and clearly

+ **Rose quartz:** a classic stone for sparking love, warmth, and trust

+ **Angel aura quartz:** an all-around aid in centering your emotions and spreading intense joy and positivity

CHAPTER 4

ENGAGING WITH YOUR GUARDIAN ANGELS

It's far from uncommon to hear people talk about guardian angels. "Your guardian angel must be looking out for you"—sound familiar at all? Still, how much do you know about the role your guardian angel plays in your life? And have you ever communicated with your angel? It's very possible to have your guardian angels be a bigger part of your life—all you need is to know more about them and how to receive and send messages. So let's dive in and make that happen.

WHAT ARE GUARDIAN ANGELS?

Guardian angels as a concept are ancient, traceable through centuries of history and many locales and religions. In essence, your guardian angel is assigned to you to protect, watch, and guide you throughout your life. Yep, that means from birth to death, your guardian angel is watching out and providing a nudge, protection, or messages when you need help most. Whether or not you recognize those signals and nudges is another story, though.

In the Christian context, guardian angels' ultimate goal is to guide your soul to salvation, leading you along the way when you need direction. But even for those who remove the element of organized religion from their angel connections, guardian angels are there as your spiritual protectors, emotional cornerstones, and wise guides, specifically supporting you throughout your life. Your guardian angel is already there and knows about you. Even if you haven't reached out yet, your angel is already working on your behalf.

Another thing to keep in mind: many who communicate with angels these days believe that we each have multiple guardian angels, not just one. One may be focused on a particular aspect of your life, while another focuses elsewhere. It's up to you, as you begin to reach out and connect, to learn how many guardian angels you have and who they are.

HOW DOES YOUR GUARDIAN ANGEL SEND SIGNS?

There are many ways your guardian angel might already be reaching out, sending you a message, or showing up in your subconscious. With time and practice, you'll find it much easier to recognize these moments.

Richard Webster outlines some of these methods perfectly in his book *Angels for Beginners.* He includes "knowing," dreams, synchronicities and coincidences, thoughts and feelings, intuition, and prayer. Let's dig a bit deeper into some of these and how you might experience them.

A sense of **knowing** sounds vague and confusing, and in some ways it is (vague, at least). But some people may experience a sudden and unexplainable *knowledge* that their guardian angel is with them and protecting them. If this thought or understanding crosses your mind, don't just dismiss it. Reflect on it, and realize it's likely to be knowledge placed in your thoughts by your angel.

Coincidences and synchronicities are events that we often attribute to the divine, unknown, or paranormal. So it may be less of a surprise that these can certainly be signals from your guardian angel. A strong coincidence—such as thinking about your guardian angel and then reading the angel's name in a book moments later—isn't something to disregard either. Coincidences are often less *coincidental* than we might imagine. If you think, "Huh, what an odd coincidence," it's more than likely someone is sending you a message.

You experience thousands of **thoughts and feelings** each day, most of which are completely your own and do not represent messages from your guardian angel. However, if you experience an unusual thought that feels distinct from your normal pattern, or a burst of creative inspiration you can't attribute to your own mind, you could be looking at a hint from your guardian. It's worth following those thoughts to see where they lead.

If you've ever had a strong hunch about something, your **intuition** is putting in work. Sometimes, these moments of strong intuition aren't coming from your own subconscious but have been placed there by your guardian angel. Have a feeling you shouldn't go out one night, then hear there was an accident on your route home? That intuition kept you safe, and you can probably thank your guardian angel for it.

Dreams are a major way your guardian angel will send you messages. Dreams aren't really as random as they often appear. There are often messages embedded in your dreams, whether they're messages from your own subconscious or from a guardian angel or other presence. Because dreams can float away so easily when you wake up, it's extra important to keep a dream journal right by your bed to jot notes in when you awaken.

HOW CAN YOU ENGAGE WITH YOUR GUARDIAN ANGEL?

So you know now that you might already be getting subtle signals and messages from your guardian angel in numerous ways. But what if you want to create a bond and be the one to reach out? Truth be told, connecting this way is probably easier than noticing your angel's (often subtle) messages!

1. Pray: If there's a religious component to your angel communications—even a spiritual element not tied to an organized religion—it's a safe bet that targeted, open-minded prayer will put you in touch. At the very least, praying will let your guardian angel(s) know you want to connect.

2. Write in your angel journal: We'll include an exercise for this activity later in this chapter, but yes—writing notes and intentions in your angel journal is a perfect way to reach out!

3. Designate and create an altar space: Having a small but dedicated space where you sit to talk, write, or send gratitude to your guardian angel will be highly effective in getting you connected. It's also a space where you can place items that remind you of your angels or that help you contact them safely (like crystals, sacred objects, and so on).

4. Meditate and get thoughtful: Sitting in quiet reflection and contemplating your desire to reach out, meditating, or sending positive thoughts and feelings will all be beneficial.

ACTIVE EXERCISE

Learning Your Guardian Angel's Name

Starting off with the basics, as you seek to build a strong connection with your guardian angels, it's important to learn their names so you know whom to address, whether out loud, internally, or in a written note. Learning your angels' names is also a sign of respect. Asking to know their names and using their names respectfully will show your angels how serious you are about the relationship you're building. You wouldn't make a human friend and just never learn their name, right?

When you first start angel communications, the first one you're likely to hear from is your primary guardian angel. This angel is the closest to you and therefore always around and ready to receive a message. So assume in this exercise that's the angel you're contacting.

There are several ways you might ask your guardian angel's name, but this is a great method to try first.

1. Find a space to be at peace, relaxed, and relatively uninterrupted. Perhaps you're in the park, your yard, or a comfortable spot in your home.

2. Relax your mind and sit restfully for a while, perhaps thirty minutes or so. During this time, if you're having conscious thoughts, focus them on your guardian angel, what your angel may do for you and may have been doing all your life, and your desire to know your angel better.

3. Pay attention to any thoughts or feelings that arise that may actually be your angel speaking or connecting with you. If a feather floats by, or the sunlight hits in an interesting way, note that this is likely a signal that the angel is nearby and listening.

4. Think or say aloud, "Guardian angel, I would love to connect with you. When you're ready to share it, I feel it would deepen our connection if I learned your name."

5. Pay attention and wait to see whether you hear or intuit a name in the moment. Know that the angel may not simply share this right away, or you may not be able to hear or sense the answer immediately. Pay attention in the moment, thank the angel, and go on about your day.

6. In the coming days, pay closer attention. It's likely your angel will share their name in time, whether during a dream or in waking life. If you continually see the same name repeated in various mediums and on various days (perhaps on a billboard, then on some movie credits, in a podcast or an audiobook, or on a flyer on the street, and so on), make note of the name. The more times in short succession that you notice this name, the more likely it is that your angel is sharing their name with you.

JOURNALING EXERCISE

Writing to Your Guardian Angels

One simple and highly effective way to reach out and make contact is to write a letter. And in this case, write directly to your guardian angel. This is something you can do anytime you feel inclined to share some thoughts with your angel or have a direct question or request you want to lay out on paper. But writing a letter can also be a great first step in building your relationship.

So, grab your angel journal or a nice piece of stationery. Write the letter exactly as you would to a human loved one. Start with a greeting, referring to the guardian angel by name if you've learned it, or simply as "guardian angel" if you haven't. Use respectful, joyful language, remembering the many things your angel has done for you without your knowledge.

Express gratitude for the angel's presence and support, always. Especially if you're making a request, it's key to show how appreciative you are. Feel free to write out the questions you want guidance on or the problems you're facing. After all, your guardian angels are there to love, support, and lead you through life, whatever is happening. Though they may not be able to fix everything you're dealing with—some challenges are lessons we need—your guardian angels can often lead you down the right path or fill you with the emotional resolve to take the next step.

As with any letter, write a kind closing and sign your name. If you feel inclined to, meditate while holding your letter, hold a crystal in your other hand while writing, or write the letter at your angel altar. Any of these will help you fully connect to that guardian angel. Then simply tuck the letter in a safe place or carefully burn it while giving thanks and wait for a reply, however it may come.

Create an Angel Altar

This step is totally up to you, and there's a chance that it feels like "too much." That's OK, though you also may find that the longer you're in contact with your angels the more you feel open to the idea of creating an altar. Altars don't need to be religious or "witchy," though they certainly can be! At its heart, an altar is a sacred space where you can go to connect with the divine; contact ancestors, angels, or other beings; or meditate on a deeper level. For some, an altar may be a space for performing spells or cleansing sacred items, but this isn't a requirement. Really, it's your space, which means it's yours to create as you prefer it and as it will best serve you.

For your starter altar, all you'll need is this:

+ A flat space, safe from nosy pets or kids

+ Items that make you feel spiritually aware and connected

That's really it! What can those items be? Well, for starters:

- + Candles
- + Incense
- + Crystals
- + Small ornaments or trinkets
- + Your angel journal
- + Photos of angels or loved ones

- + Beloved keepsakes or items that remind you of a passed loved one
- + Angel cards, tarot cards, or oracle cards
- + Sage or other significant herbs
- + Items tied to your religion or faith (a rosary, a Buddha statue, or any number of other items)

The best part is that none of these is required—anything goes! Once you put it all together, your altar should simply feel like a spiritually significant, safe place where you can sit to write in your angel journal, meditate, or make contact. Place your chosen items in a way that's pleasing to you, making sure any candles have room to burn safely. Then start using this space whenever you feel called to or for any of the exercises you try from this book!

CHAPTER 5

ANGEL JOURNALING

Does every chapter of this book technically include some recommendations and exercises for journaling? Why, yes! Still, angel journaling is so key, it's worth digging into the topic a bit more in a focused chapter. Here, I'll touch a bit more on some of the ways your angel journal can be put to use, but I'll also highlight more journal-based exercises and question prompts to help you dig deeper as you continue on your path.

HOW CAN ANGEL JOURNALING SUPPORT AND GUIDE YOU?

1. It's a space to look back on and see how your perspectives, feelings, and desires have evolved over time. If you start answering the prompts and following the exercises from the beginning of this book to the end, I promise that when you look back, you'll realize how much you've learned and developed on your path to connecting with loving divine messengers.

2. You'll have a record of the requests you've made and questions you've asked your angels. If you keep track of each of the major asks you put out there, or the big questions you pose, you will have a way to look back and see that even if the angels didn't solve the problem or answer the question exactly as you had hoped or expected, they handled the situation or guided you toward a path that was ultimately right for you and your growth. Seeing your dreams and worries written out, and looking back later to see the unique ways your angel guides led and supported you, can only serve to enhance your belief and connection.

3. You can record dreams or passing, near-subconscious thoughts that come up during meditation. These are often messages or signals from your angels, and keeping them in one spot can help you recall them later.

4. You can track patterns. If you start recording each time you experience a synchronicity, an angel number, a unique sign, and so on, you'll be able to watch for recurring messages and get a better sense of what angels are communicating to you.

5. You won't be at risk of forgetting things! No matter whether it's dreams, your requests to angels, which angel you're communicating with during a particular week, or something else, we're all prone to forgetting things. You may lose track of what you've already asked of your angels. If you note everything on paper along the way, you'll have a record that will prevent you from losing this information.

JOURNALING EXERCISE
How Will You Use Your Angel Journal?

Reflect on the following questions in your journal, so you have a paper reminder:

✦ Have you ever been one to keep a diary or journal?

✦ Do you find if beneficial to write down your thoughts, concerns, dreams, and so on?

✦ How have you already been using your angel journal?

✦ How might you expand its use to help you grow in your practice even more?

✦ Since you've started journaling, have you noticed any patterns, dream messages, or signals?

Starting a Tracker

Open to a blank two-page spread of your journal and label it with a heading along the lines of "Signs and Feelings Tracker." This will be a record of signs and signals that you can continually update and refer back to. The point is to jot down some of the main ways you think your angel is reaching out to you and then note the date, location, and any key details each time you experience that signal again. As the weeks and months add up, you can circle back and see patterns. For example, you might realize, "Oh, wow, my guardian angel really likes to use scents and sounds to connect—I'll keep that in mind when I'm looking for messages."

So, set up your tracker any way that makes sense to you. You could draw a table, with columns for each type of sign or signal you experience, and add new ones as they arise. Or get creative and do it your own way!

Start by writing out some of the signs and signals you already notice, either occasionally or often. Start adding quick notes each time you catch this sign again, or add a new category when you think you notice a new kind of signal.

Here are some potential signs and signals your angel may be sending:

+ Feathers, especially in odd spots

+ Repetition of a name—probably the angel's!

+ Bright or unique paths of light at unexpected times

+ Light sounds, like bells or chimes (not constant or annoyingly repetitive—again, see a doctor if you experience that kind of sound)

+ A beautiful scent passing by with no clear source

+ Regularly seeing the same animal, plant, or something else that reminds you of a passed loved one

+ Candles flickering at significant moments

+ Frequently hearing a beloved or significant song

+ Repeated dreams

ACTIVE EXERCISE

Beautify Your Angel Journal

Decorating your angel journal is by no means a requirement for starting the journal or communicating with angels—but gosh, is it fun, and you may be more inclined to pick up your journal after you've beautified it. After all, if you put work into making it pretty and eye-catching, it'll be on your mind more and more exciting to use.

Take your basic angel journal and get to work making it look creative and beautiful— totally reflective of you, your angels, and your connection. This could mean so many things. Perhaps you'll adhere pictures of your loved ones and ancestors to the covers to remind you of the people watching you. Perhaps you'll collage the outside and even inside covers with clippings, images, and fun art that reminds of you of angels and spirituality. You could incorporate things such as ribbons, lace, or feathers to enhance your collage, too.

Step things up and add a lock, or attach a tassel you can use to tie your journal closed. You could use wax to create an emblem on the front, or create a little pocket to hold a pen or bookmark. Better yet, install a ribbon bookmark to help you open your journal to the right page. If, when you finish your wild creative adventure, the journal is bursting with images, scraps, and lovely little treasures, you've done some great work. Some people, of course, will prefer to keep a simple, plain journal. But others of us like a little pizzazz in our writing supplies—and it might delight your angels too!

CHAPTER 6

EXPLORING INTUITION

Intuition is probably a concept you're familiar with, at least very generally. Some people, especially practicing psychics and mediums, rely heavily on the power of intuiting important information about the people around them. But for most of us, intuition is a bit like background noise—something we have circling around us somewhere but tune out and don't pay much mind to.

Intuition is now considered an important psychological concept and has been covered in many studies and psychological journals for decades, though the recent evidence uncovered by scientists has been much more confident. In an article for *Psychology Today*, Francis P. Cholle outlines some simple definitions of intuition, which I think are a perfect starting point for digging into a more spiritual take on the idea. He says:

> Instinct is our innate inclination toward a particular behavior (as opposed to a learned response).

> A gut feeling—or a hunch—is a sensation that appears quickly in consciousness (noticeable enough to be acted on if one chooses to) without us being fully aware of the underlying reasons for its occurrence.

Intuition is a process that gives us the ability to know something directly without analytic reasoning, bridging the gap between the conscious and non-conscious parts of our mind, and also between instinct and reason.[7]

When you go a step further, deepening your intuition and willingness to listen to those instincts can actually help open you up to receive the messages your angels are sending and expand your connection with them. Everyone's intuition works and acts differently, and there's no one right way to intuit information or signs. Author and professional intuitive Tanya Carroll Richardson notes,

> Your intuition is as unique as you are. You might receive intuitive information by sensing the emotions and energy of those around you, or you might hear a gentle voice in your mind, or see images appear like a photograph or mini movie in your head, or you might get large chunks of information suddenly planted in your brain like a download from heaven—or maybe you experience a few or even all four of these methods. Perhaps you have prophetic dreams or receive a ton of synchronicities. We all have a sixth sense, but beyond that the way we each experience and absorb information from our intuition can be very different.[8]

You might notice that her list of ways your intuited information can appear aligns in many ways with some of the examples of methods angels use to reach out—such as dream signals, images appearing in your mind, hearing a voice or sound in your mind, and so on. So, it's no surprise that learning about and following your intuition can help you as you explore the relationships you want to build with angels.

Here are some key points to remember when it comes to your intuition and spiritual growth.

----

7   Francis P. Cholle, "What Is Intuition, and How Do We Use It?," *Psychology Today*, August 31, 2011.
8   Tanya Carroll Richardson, "10 Things You Probably Don't Know About Your Intuition," *Llewellyn*, November 26, 2018.

We all have intuition already, but there's always room for growth. While we're all born with some level of intuition (or instinct, as we might think of it), some are given much more—or more awareness of it and willingness to listen to it—while others of us may be more logical and resist listening to intuition and impulses that seem not to come from a place of reasoning and analytics. However, with time, patience, and practice, anyone can build their intuitive skills and use them to deepen their connections with themselves, their loved ones, and divine beings (such as angels!).

Sensitivity and empathy can be linked to intuition. If you're a highly sensitive person (HSP) or strongly empathetic, you may notice already that your intuition is stronger or that you're more inclined to notice it and listen to it. HSPs are great at picking up the subtle cues in the people and spaces around them, which also means they can be better at intuiting things, whether that's a message from an angel or a synchronicity that's important to notice. It's all about perception.

While improving your intuition can help you connect more with your angels, your angels can also help you improve your intuition. Yep, it's a two-way street. It's totally valid to ask your guardian angel for nudges to help encourage you to follow those intuitive hits when they appear. Basically, you're getting a second opinion, and a powerful one at that.

Using your intuition more doesn't mean you should ignore logic. Yes, you want to pay more attention to the intuitive hits you get. Perhaps you get a strong gut feeling that you should turn down a particular job offer or a chance to date someone. You might be saving yourself some pain or challenges. Or you might intuit that a particular opportunity is a great one for you. Still, remember to keep logic (and safety) in mind, too. If all the clear logical signs point toward or against something, that's worth noting and factoring into your decision as well.

How Good Is Your Intuition?

We all have some level of intuition that we're born with and that we hone or develop over time. You may already possess more intuition than you think, so pondering and answering some of these questions can help you get a sense of your intuitive skills and starting point, before you take any steps to boost your intuition.

✦ Are you particularly sensitive to the moods, feelings, and reactions of other people? Have you ever considered yourself an HSP, or have you been told that you might be one?

✦ Are you easily overwhelmed by crowds, intense emotions, or heavy experiences?

✦ Have you ever made a choice that went against your typical reactions, simply because of a "gut feeling" or instinct?

✦ Do you ever feel "nudges" or pushes toward or away from someone you meet?

✦ Do you walk into a new space and instantly feel a good or bad "vibe" about it?

✦ Do you ever hear a voice or see a physical manifestation giving you a message?

✦ Are your choices driven more by logic and analytical thinking or by sensations, feelings, and gut reactions?

✦ When you're faced with a challenge, do you immediately problem-solve, or do you experiment with potential solutions and wait for one to show itself as the best?

✦ Do the decisions you make based on instinct tend to pan out better or worse than those you make based on planning and logic?

Small Ways to Improve Your Intuition

Becoming more intuitive or an expert intuitive does not happen overnight. For most, getting there will take some time, patience, and practice. But the benefits you can reap—from better decision-making and life satisfaction to clearer understanding of the people around you or a stronger connection with angels—are all worth the effort, if you're willing to try! So, experiment with some of these tactics for improving your intuition over time.

1. Meditate often! Meditation seems to—and just might—help with everything. Meditation can clear and open your mind, making you more receptive to intuitive hits.

2. Track and record your dreams. Often, they are places where your intuition shines. Keeping track of patterns and signs in your dreams is a great way to start learning about the intuitive messages you receive.

3. Be open-minded. Frankly, you probably already are if you're seeking out relationships with your angels. However, the more open you can be to the idea of anything being possible, the more those things will work for you.

4. Ask your guardian angel for help! When you write or speak to your guardian angel, mention that you're trying to improve your intuition so you're better able to communicate with them, and ask if they can offer insights or support on this journey.

5. Hone your five other senses. Calling intuition your "sixth sense" is fair (and traditional), but working to appreciate and use to their fullest your other five senses will help you pay more attention to that sixth one. Savor flavors and scents, touch things to explore new textures, listen carefully, and watch with open eyes. Value every sense you have, including that elusive sixth one.

6. Be outside as much as possible. Being in nature and greenery whenever you have a chance is beneficial for just about everything, and your intuition has plenty to gain from being outside.

7. Track and record your intuitive moments and how you responded to them. If you have a gut instinct or a moment of intuition, make note of it, whether in your angel journal or a more focused journal. Then, when that situation plays out, look back and record the result. Whether you followed the intuition or not, was that the right choice? What does that show you about the strength of your intuitive power?

CHAPTER 7

ANGEL NUMBERS FOR BEGINNERS

You may have been reading along so far thinking, "Why isn't she talking about angel numbers?" You're right to ask that question! We've waited this long because the topic deserves to have a whole chapter dedicated to it. Now that you have more general familiarity with angels, guardians, and some forms of signs they may send, it's time to dig into a big category many angel communicators and practitioners use often: angel numbers.

Like many of the key subtopics discussed in these pages, this one has been covered elsewhere at much more length—in full books, in fact. Remember, this chapter just scratches the surface and gives you practical knowledge, so that if you do feel called to angel numbers, you can continue your research and dig in even deeper after reading what's included here.

So what are angel numbers? Among the many ways angels send signs and messages, using numbers is a biggie—to the extent that people have dedicated their lives and time to deciphering the meanings behind each number, just so newbies can have a better understanding as they dive in.

If you're always seeing the same numbers popping up—on your receipts, when you wake up in the middle of the night and check the time, when you check your car's mileage, when you book appointments, when you glance at the clock, in your Social

Security number and your bank accounts—you're probably being clued in to a message from an angel. And these messages may have been arriving for quite a while without your picking up on them. Sure, if you wake up every night right at 4:04 and 6:15, you will probably notice eventually. But what do those numbers mean? Perhaps more than you imagine.

So, why numbers? Mystic Michaela offers a great answer in *The Angel Numbers Book*:

> Numbers occur in every place both on and beyond earth. Their patterns are found in everything that surrounds you, governing the planet's movements, the weather, sound, light, and even your own DNA. Number patterns exist in the most infinite reaches of your imagination and inward to the microcosm of your being. Because they are universal, they are the perfect medium for sending messages.[9]

Essentially, no matter where you live on earth, what language you speak, or how much of a connection you have to the divine, your spirituality, or your guardians, you will encounter numbers and patterns in your life—from measures of age, time, and distance to elements of our day-to-day such as bank account balances and phone battery life. The angels are smart: they use those numbers to send signals and share wisdom. We just have to learn to recognize those signals.

It's one thing to see the number four a couple of times in a day. It's extremely common and you probably see that number most days. It might stand out to you more than usual, and it's good to take note when you do see it. But those sightings are probably not on the level of synchronicity. However, seeing longer numbers or repeated strings of numbers again and again in unique ways? Now it's time to take note. Every time you glance at a clock it's 4:44? Then you check your bank account and you have $444 available? That's something to reflect on!

---

9   Mystic Michaela, *The Angel Numbers Book* (Avon, MA: Adams Media, 2021), 11.

As Mystic Michaela adds, "Synchronicity is the moment when spiritual incidents are interconnected, yet not logically so. When a coincidence becomes an unreasonable explanation, synchronicity is at play."[10] Angels love to use synchronicities to open your eyes to messages they're trying to send. And with your newfound knowledge and experience, you're ready to notice, right?

THE CARDINAL NUMBERS

Let's first note the single digit numbers, zero through nine. It's atypical that a message will be built of just one of these numbers. While they have meanings attached to them, angels know we see these numbers all the time and won't associate much significance with seeing the number seven a few times. It's when you get a few numbers paired together that you notice—which is the reason angels will rely on those pairings to get in touch.

Seeing a sequence of the same cardinal number repeated a few times—for example "222" or "5555"—is perhaps even more significant. The more times the number is repeated, the more of an emphasis the angels are putting on that message. This is the way that the meanings of the cardinal numbers can come into play.

Let's explore some meanings:

Zeroes: Enjoy fresh starts and new beginnings.

Ones: A great sign from the angels and universe that you should proceed. You have support, so it's time to manifest what you're dreaming of.

Twos: A signal of alignment and balance; it may be time to find a beneficial partnership, or put one to work.

Threes: You are channeling great creativity; use it!

----
10   Mystic Michaela, *The Angel Numbers Book*, 13.

Fours: This is the perfect time to ground, center, and find stability—or new opportunity!

Fives: Big changes are coming, and it's time to brace for them and lean in.

Sixes: You are in a space of love and compassion—big-time. Enjoy it. (That's right! In angel numbers, repeated sixes constitute a positive, loving message, not something to fear superstitiously.)

Sevens: You have luck on your side, so invest, try something new, or take the leap you've considered.

Eights: Many see these as a divine message, perhaps a contact from a passed loved one. It can also be a message of abundance and success.

Nines: Because nine is the final cardinal number, it often signifies the end of a chapter or some other conclusion. This ending doesn't have to be negative; perhaps it's time to move on to the next phase of life or part of your journey.

Now, are these meanings 100 percent conclusive, set in stone, and all-encompassing? Of course not! Just because nines indicate an ending doesn't mean it's always a massive one. Perhaps it's an angel signaling agreement with your decision to end a friendship or move to a new place. Threes often signal creativity but have also been said to reflect joy and positivity. And these are just a few examples.

So, sometimes when you see a repeated number or sequence, the meaning may be totally clear. Perhaps you're deciding whether to start a business partnership and start seeing tons of repeated twos. Easy interpretation, right? But at other times, perhaps you'll see the numbers and not be quite sure of their meaning. It's possible the circumstances of the message haven't shown up in your life yet, or they're not too clear. You can always ask your angels for clarity, or you can just wait it out and see whether more understanding will be revealed in time.

WHAT ABOUT MIXES OF NUMBERS?

Though it's more common to talk about repeated series such as "1111" or "444," repeatedly seeing the same mix of numbers is also significant—you just might need to parse out the message a bit more!

For example, maybe you keep seeing "319," again and again. On the clock, on receipts, in phone numbers, and so on. This could be a cue to dig a little deeper. The number three often signals creative pursuits and endeavors; ones are about manifesting new things with support from your guides; and nines are about endings and moving forward. Piecing it together and looking at your life, where does this message make sense? Perhaps you're considering leaving your current job and pursuing something more risky but creative. Here's your sign: nines to represent the end of something, threes to say that this is a creative moment, and ones to tell you that your angels have your back and support you in manifesting this dream.

Take this logic and system and apply it to any number sequence that's been reoccurring for you. You might be surprised at how quickly a message is revealed.

HOW DO LOCATIONS AND TIMES FACTOR IN?

Sometimes you'll see an angel number at a totally random moment during your day. This could just be the easiest way for your angel to get that message to you or to reiterate the message. However, pay attention to more significant circumstances, too. Maybe you're driving down the road actively thinking about a huge life decision when you see the repeated number on a billboard or license plate. That's synchronicity in timing. Do you keep hearing and seeing the same number pattern in your dreams? You know that angels use dreams to communicate. Have you been feeling as though you've hit rock bottom, and then you start seeing the same numbers over and over? These are all significant events to track! Pay more attention, and you'll start realizing these messages are all around you, waiting to be noticed. Angels aren't shy about trying to reach you.

Considering Numerology and Angel Numbers

Before you dive deeper and start tracking some potential messages of your own, take a moment to pull out your angel journal and record some thoughts and feelings about these questions. Again, recording your attitudes and perceptions is helpful so you can get a sense of your perspectives on something now versus down the road when all of this becomes more a part of your life. You might look back in a year or two at what you've recorded and realize, "Wow, I've learned and grown so much in my practice, I see angel numbers all the time now!"

✦ What are your thoughts on numerology, angel numbers, and the like at this point?

✦ Do you believe in the significance of birthdays, astrology, or other elements of numerology?

✦ Have you ever read or heard about angel numbers before?

✦ Have you ever noticed repeating numbers in your life and ignored them because you didn't understand their significance?

✦ Have you seen numbers and ascribed significance to them yourself? Were you surprised to realize you may have been right about the meaning?

Diving into an Angel Number Message

This isn't an exercise you can necessarily do right this moment; instead, it's one to return to whenever you do start seeing a recurring sequence of numbers pop up in your life. If you start seeing similar numbers or repeating numbers, make note of them in your angel journal (even just a quick note of the number and date is plenty: "Saw something odd—3:33 when I woke up the last two nights" is so helpful). Then—aha!—when you see that number again a week later, you have a note reminding you that this isn't the first time or perhaps even the second time that the number is popping up. Once you're confident that a number is a message, you can come back to this exercise. Follow these questions and steps to get a better sense of what the message might mean. You can even make notes right here in your book.

✦ Number or numbers I've seen repeatedly:

✦ How many times I've seen the number so far:

✦ Times and places I've seen the number:

✦ Is it a repeated number (e.g., "333") or a unique sequence (e.g., "458")?

✦ What are typical meanings for this number or these numbers? (according to the list set out earlier in the chapter and any additional research you've done)

✦ Do the locations or times when I encountered this number add to or influence the message? Were these locations or times particularly significant?

✦ Current life circumstances, challenges, or questions this message may relate to:

✦ What I think this message says:

Remember, when it comes to making a final call on the meaning of the message in that last prompt on the worksheet, you're using your intuition and the clues you've gathered from research. Tracking number messages on a worksheet like this one is a great way to use a combination of logic and intuition to discover what is being said and what the message means for you.

CHAPTER 8

EMBRACING THE POWER OF MANIFESTATION

As with many of the key topics we're exploring in this book, the idea of manifesting, or the law of attraction, is likely something you've heard about before—or perhaps you even practice manifestation already. Whether or not you do now, I'm hoping to show you the enormous power of manifesting and how it can help you create the life of your dreams. Manifestation can also go hand in hand with your angel communication, and that's a huge bonus as well.

Manifestation is a major hot-button topic these days, covered thoroughly across mainstream lifestyle platforms from Oprah to HuffPost. The topic has also seen a rise in popularity on TikTok and is moving more and more into the public eye. And it's no wonder, really. We're struggling with a lot, as a society and as a world; seeking positive, helpful ways to get some good things in life isn't so strange. There's no shortage of people out there successfully using manifestation to live their dream life—which means there's also no shortage of tips and methods for how to do it yourself.

The core concept here is that if you think positively and actively about something you want and desire, you will draw it to you. Whether that's money and prosperity, love, success, peace, or happiness, the theories maintain that all you have to do is think aspirationally about the things you want, and they will, in a bit of time, become real. Amazing, right?

Of course, manifestation can't do anything and everything. You can't will away disease or war with positive thinking; some problems really do require outside intervention or community. But, again and again, people are proving that simply by thinking confidently and positively about the life they want (sometimes writing down the qualities of this life as well), they manifest it into existence. That dream job, perfect partner, or amazing opportunity shows up, as if by magic. Positive thinking, in fact, is a bit like magic—the kind we have ready access to. And making use of this magic, especially to create the lives we want and deserve, is as noble an activity as any.

HOW TO MANIFEST: THE BASICS

Ask ten people how to manifest and you will get ten different answers, all with the same core. Yes, you attract the things you want by thinking or writing about them. But while some will tell you manifestation is as simple as that, other people will add extra steps. Really, I think it's about finding what works for you and what feels right. Some guidance may seem counterintuitive to you, and other guidance may seem appropriate—follow your intuition.

In its simplest form, manifesting is just defining your goals and ambitions clearly for yourself and then dedicating positive thoughts and energy toward them. I'm definitely a proponent of continuing to put in physical steps toward those goals, rather than sitting back and waiting for them to materialize—but some prefer that option. Either way, it's not at all surprising that it works wonders for many people to simply get a clear view of their goals and direct their focus and energy toward them.

Want to try manifestation yourself? Start by visualizing your dream life or the thing you want badly right now. Perhaps that's a new, fulfilling job; a romantic connection; supportive friends; healed relationships with loved ones; a new place to live; a pet;

financial success and stability; travel—the list goes on and on. For now, focus on one goal to start with, perhaps something that feels like an important beginning for your dream life.

Then, start dedicating good mental space to that goal. Think only positive thoughts surrounding it. Use affirmation-style phrases rather than negative ones (the next chapter will focus on affirmations; essentially, you want to aim for thoughts such as "I am becoming financially stable," rather than thoughts like "I will never be financially stable"). Think about the goal as though it's a guarantee, a given. Leave negativity out of it. Put these positive thoughts out there whenever you can—driving in traffic, cooking dinner, getting ready for bed.

If doing so feels powerful to you, write down the manifestation as well, whether in the pages of this book, in a journal, or on a scrap of paper. Often, making a thought physical can give it more power. Then, be patient. Watch for opportunities to come to you. And don't turn down possibilities that may have surprising outcomes. If you're manifesting an amazing relationship and someone asks you out on a date, it's time to say yes, rather than turning the person down for a silly reason. You may be looking at the product of your manifestation and the perfect partner for you, even if you wouldn't have given the person a chance at another time.

HOW CAN ANGELS BE INVOLVED?

Considering the things we've covered that angels are able to do for you—from giving you signs when you're on the right or wrong path to actually bringing amazing things into your life—it shouldn't be surprising that angels can serve as manifestation boosters. So why not incorporate them into your life-improvement journey?

1. Angel numbers are associated with manifestation by many. In particular, the numbers "111" and "444" are often connected with manifesting your dream life, so if you start seeing these numbers popping up, you're getting a sign from your angels that they're on your side for this manifestation.

2. Use your angel journal! If this is the perfect space to record interactions and messages from angels, it's also the right spot to record what you want to manifest. Your angels will see it just the same, and step in to guide or support you where they can.

3. You can ask your angels for help! If you're asking your guardian angel for support with a challenge in life or for wisdom on an issue, why not ask your angel to give you a boost on your manifesting journey? There's no shortage of positive, compassionate, loving power coming right to you from your angels. They'll help whenever they can.

JOURNALING EXERCISE
Manifestation Worksheet

Use the following worksheet-style page and prompts to fill in as you attempt to manifest something beautiful in your life. Though it may seem silly sometimes to write things down so specifically, you'll be shocked at the power of stating your goals and intentions so you can channel all your good vibes toward them (and your angels can, too).

Today's date is: ....

✦ I want to manifest:

....

....

....

✦ This will help me find happiness and contentment in my life for this reason:

✦ I will use these affirmations when I think or speak about this manifestation:

✦ I will take this concrete step toward my vision of my best life:

✦ I will ask my guardian angels to guide me on this manifesting path by . . . [*journaling, asking the angels directly, meditating, and so on*]:

Manifestation Meditation

Here is a simple guided meditation that is perfect to help you on your journey to manifest amazing, joyous things in your life. As with any meditation, start by finding a comfortable position in a quiet, distraction-free space.

Begin with a clear vision in your mind of the goal you're working to manifest. Take a deep, cleansing breath in. Tune in to your body and its sensations, noticing the floor beneath you and the way your legs or feet touch it.

Breathe in deeply again, holding for four seconds, and then exhale for four seconds. As you release your breath, tense your whole body, feeling your muscles contract. Then, taking another deep breath in, release all the tension in your body as you exhale once again.

On one final deep breath, find your center—the space in your body closest to your heart, soul, and vital life energy. Breathe in, reflecting positive feelings and energy for that space and the energy that keeps you moving.

Now, turn your attention to the goal you've kept in your mind's eye. This important image is the thing you dream of, whatever it is you plan to attract to your life. Sit quietly, focusing your attention on a *vivid, clear picture of exactly* what you want.

Within this image in your mind's eye, step inside your own body, embodying the space and accepting it as your own reality. Fully see yourself physically living this version of your life, embodying this version of yourself that has the things you dream of. Sit peacefully in this visualization for as long as you can, letting it take over your thoughts and experiencing it as real. Explore the sensations of your body in this envisioned reality. Enjoy the positive, happy feelings this new reality offers, letting your body fill with gratitude for this reality and its gifts, for the way it makes you feel.

Take these good feelings in, letting them fill you up with warm, light, beautiful joy. Explore the way this reality of abundance makes you feel—every positive feeling—seeing it all as a warm, bright light encompassing you and filling you up from the inside out.

These things are coming to you in your own right and time. Accept this truth, taking it for your own and acknowledging that the things you envision for your future are yours to claim.

This will be done. You can give in now, trusting that in time the things you envision and manifest will come to you. Channeling all the good feelings you've explored, take a few final deep breaths to end your meditation. Come back to your body when you're comfortable, and open your eyes. Thank the universe, your angels, and any other guides for the gifts they have given, and those yet to come.

CHAPTER 9

EXPLORING INTENTIONS, AFFIRMATIONS, AND MANTRAS

Intentions, affirmations, and mantras—all in the same conceptual family—involve using positive words and thoughts to improve your life. These activities are closely connected to manifesting. But by creating and using intentions, affirmations, and mantras, you're simply grounding yourself in words and feelings that inspire positive change, rather than specifically *bringing* the change into your life (manifesting is a bit more active).

Because intentions, affirmations, and mantras are so closely connected, it seems worthwhile to dig more specifically into them, how they can help you, and how you can tie them to your angelic communications.

FIRST UP, SETTING INTENTIONS

When you set an intention, you're simply putting more stock in the fact that you plan and intend to make something happen. Rather than thinking vaguely that you wish your life was better, for example, you're getting specific and intentional—so that you can work toward that positive future, through any means you prefer.

Setting a clear intention forces you to look directly at the things you want and the goals you're striving for, and forces you to take accountability for the actions and choices that

EXPLORING INTENTIONS, AFFIRMATIONS, AND MANTRAS

will take you there. Setting an intention makes you a more purposeful player in your own life; rather than being content to sit back and hope idly for something, you are being direct and intentional about the goals you have and the ways you'll achieve them.

What do intentions look like? Almost anything, really! As long as you focus closely on what you want and can work toward, you're setting an intention by putting it in words, whether you speak the words out loud or write them down on paper. The only key qualities for an intention are clarity (it should not be complicated or confusing), simplicity, and positive wording.

For example:

+ This is the year I'll make time and money for travel.
+ I'm going to make sure to find a job I'm passionate about in the next [ ] months.
+ I am ready to end this relationship and find myself.
+ I am going to put myself out there and make new friendships.
+ I'm going to start dating and be open to people I might have overlooked before.

And so on! There's no wrong way to set an intention if you follow these few basic principles.

NEXT UP, EXPLORING AFFIRMATIONS

Also highly popular in the life-improvement world these days, positive affirmations are proving to have great benefits for our mental well-being. It only makes sense. Rather than beating yourself up with words and thoughts such as "I'll never be good enough" or "I'm a failure" (ideas that are basically guaranteed to keep you in a negative, unsuccessful mindset), you're filling your mind with thoughts like "I can handle anything that life throws at me" or "I am capable of getting through this and finding a happy life." It's no surprise that keeping your mind and thoughts positive and affirming helps you get through each day, accomplish more, and actually push yourself into that better life you're seeking.

Though affirmations are very similar to and perhaps seemingly interchangeable with mantras, the history and background of the two differentiates them best. In the words of an article from *Integrative Nutrition*:

> Positive affirmations were developed in the 1970's by neuroscientists, incorporating a modern understanding of psychotherapy and linguistics in order to consciously rewire thought patterns towards more desired outcomes. Affirmations can be stated anytime and tend to be complete sentences addressing something we wish to have or be as if we already have it in the present moment.[11]

I'll get into the history of mantras in a moment, but know that they're a much older concept. That doesn't mean, though, that one or the other is better or worse or that you shouldn't try both!

Positive affirmations can sound like this:

+ I have immense value and deserve great things.
+ I am loved and seen.
+ I am bringing success toward me.
+ I am smart and competent.
+ My life has meaning and purpose, and I strive to see that every day.

No matter in what area of your life you need that self-support, the tone of the affirmation is always the same: affirming. Not a surprise there! The idea is to infuse positive, healthy feelings about yourself into your conscious and subconscious thought patterns, rather than let yourself be bombarded by the negative.

---

11   Danielle Kerendian, "Mantras vs. Affirmations: What's the Difference?," *Integrative Nutrition*, August 10, 2016.

FINALLY, WHAT ABOUT MANTRAS?

Mantras, like their companions intentions and affirmations, are well loved by social media, movies, and popular publications. There is no shortage of people out there saying "Start your day with mantras!" I'm here to jump on the mantra train. Tons of good can come from creating your own mantras, and just like affirmations and intentions, mantras are perfect for priming your thought processes for a cycle of positivity and self-support rather than negativity. And you know what brings you more success and joy in the long run, right?

Mantras are an art form thousands of years old in Buddhist culture, and more recently adopted by people around the world as a method for improving emotional and mental wellness. Notes Danielle Kerendian in *Integrative Nutrition*, "In the Eastern world, it is believed that words—whether thought or stated out loud—can affect our physical vibration and over time impact our perception or circumstances in a positive way. The approach—which has been used in Buddhism for thousands of years—is to repeat 'mantras' in accordance with meditation."[12]

Mantras are simple enough, in theory, though they take a bit more appreciation and cultural respect to fully understand and embody. This is a tradition steeped in meditation, so those who use mantras in their lives should be combining them with meditative practices (they go hand in hand for a reason!). And many traditional mantras are words, sounds, or syllables that may not have an English translation; they've been used by yogis for hundreds or thousands of years to create positive sensations in the mind and body. Respecting any mantra you bring into your life is important.

---

12   Kerendian, "Mantras vs. Affirmations: What's the Difference?"

Mantras:

- ✦ Interrupt negative thought patterns
- ✦ Redirect focus and thinking
- ✦ Focus energy on the positive
- ✦ Affect your brain chemistry
- ✦ Are totally personalized and customizable
- ✦ Are created by you, to help you
- ✦ Are not one-size-fits-all
- ✦ Are short, easy to remember, and simple to repeat and recite

LIFE PRACTICE EXERCISE

Setting Intentions

We've learned that intention-setting is powerful, so now let's put it into practice. This exercise can also be moved to your journal, but it is totally fine to keep your answers within the confines of your own headspace, as well as taking any notes on the spaces provided here, if that's helpful to your process.

1. Start by closing your eyes and taking a few deep breaths to enter a calm mindset.

2. In your mind's eye, reflect on the current dynamics of your life, good and bad.

3. Now, of all elements of your life, choose one goal or ambition to focus on, something you want to accomplish or achieve to improve the quality of your life. It can be anything, from making new friends, to getting out more, to finding a new place to live, or becoming financially independent.

---

4. Zeroing in on this goal, create a one-sentence intention that encapsulates it—for example, "I will master my own finances and budget and free myself from money stresses."

---

5. Now, take a look at the intention you've set. Is it clear? Simple and uncomplicated? And positively worded?

6. If so, you're on the right path. Write your intention in the box provided here and anywhere else you'll see your intention and be reminded of it. Writing your intention down somewhere significant is especially helpful because you can look back later and see that you've been able to achieve this goal and that you are ready to set a new intention.

7. Then, repeat this phrase to yourself often. Embody a mindset of positivity around this topic. Push negative thoughts away and focus on this intention: you *can* do this and make your intention a reality.

MY CURRENT INTENTION

JOURNALING EXERCISE
Crafting Perfect Affirmations and Mantras

Continuing on this self-love journey, it's time to work on creating some beautiful, powerful affirmations or mantras for yourself. If you feel more called to one or the other of the two, that's great—focus in on that calling (it's probably a bit of intuition!). If you're intrigued by both affirmations and mantras, why not try them both out and see what works best?

Start with a bit of self-reflection. In your journal, be honest with yourself. Write down some of the repeated negative self-talk you're guilty of. If there are unhealthy ideas and phrases rattling around in your head and bringing you down, it's time to acknowledge them and write them down.

Now, it's time to turn those negative, hurtful words on their heads. For each critical statement you wrote down, write a positive version to replace it—something you can repeat to yourself, write on your mirror, and so on, to make sure you're filling your mind up with positive self-love, instead of nasty self-talk that does nothing but bring you down.

Here are some examples:

IF YOU WROTE . . .	THAT CAN BECOME . . .
I am ugly and unworthy.	I recognize my unique beauty and love myself first.
I will never be successful.	I have all the tools to find success, and I will get there.
I am a failure.	I have accomplished amazing things, and do more every day.
No one likes me.	I am worthy of love and keep good connections close.
I'm behind schedule; I should be doing what everyone else is doing.	I am accomplishing everything in life at my own pace and the right time for me.

These are all great options to adopt for yourself, or you can create your own unique affirmations based on the negative self-talk you wrote down. Remember, you're reframing anything hurtful you say to yourself or feel about yourself, to remind you that you're doing great and that you can and will have the life of your dreams. However it feels right

THE ANGEL WORKBOOK

to you to create that reminder for yourself is perfect. Write down all of your affirmations in your journal.

Now, as we've seen, mantras have a tone and effect similar to those of affirmations, but mantras have a different background. The other major difference between mantras and affirmations is in the way they're structured. Affirmations tend to be a bit longer and are structured as full, encompassing sentences you can write down or repeat to yourself when you need a reminder of your value. Mantras, however, with their background in meditation and yoga, are often shorter and punchier, great for repeating many times in a row to get a satisfying mouth-to-brain rhythm going. There are countless mantras out there, from traditional Buddhist sounds and phrases to more modern options popularized in the media. And, as always, you can create your own, too (and you likely will in time). But if you need a good starting point, here are some common or simple mantras for you to try out. See how the following mantras resonate with you and the needs you have right now:

- ✦ I am not afraid to be wrong.
- ✦ I am enough.
- ✦ I am powerful.
- ✦ I choose peace.
- ✦ All is well, here and now.
- ✦ I am blessed (you can add, "with . . .")
- ✦ I am loved.

- ✦ I give love.
- ✦ I will release things I can't control.
- ✦ This too shall pass.
- ✦ I exist in this moment.
- ✦ With change comes opportunity.
- ✦ I matter.
- ✦ Progress is more important than perfection.

Choose some mantras that connect with you, or write any of your own, and list them out here or in your journal, alongside your positive affirmations. Bring these with you to your meditation practice, and bring them to mind when you need a boost of positivity or are going into a stressful situation.

✦ _____   ✦ _____

✦ _____   ✦ _____

✦ _____   ✦ _____

✦ _____   ✦ _____

✦ _____   ✦ _____

✦ _____   ✦ _____

✦ _____   ✦ _____

✦ _____   ✦ _____

✦ _____   ✦ _____

✦ _____   ✦ _____

Tying Your Angels In

Since you know that immersing angels into your life is all about accessing more love, support, compassion, and perhaps a clearer path to your best life, I'm sure it's clear why adding intention-setting, affirmations, and mantras is like adding an extra shot of espresso to your coffee—you're just expanding the positive effects of turning to your angels for help.

Also, by making lots of efforts to improve your mindset and positivity, you're showing your angels that you're learning from their advice and wisdom, rather than taking it for granted. But why not go a step further?

If you already love the idea of intentions and affirmations, tying them into your angel practice is only going to make everything better. Here are a few ways to do so:

1. When you write in your angel journal, make note of your affirmations, mantras, and intentions for the week. Anything you're really focusing on right now should be written down. That way, you can start connecting these practices to your angel work and remember what to mention to your angels.

2. When you communicate, talk about these things! If your guardian angels exist to be loving, ever-compassionate figures of support and wisdom in your life, don't you think they'll want to help with your intentions and affirmations? In conversation with your angels, if you say, "Lately, I've been focusing my energy on this intention, and I'd love any support you have," you *know* your angels will start dedicating some energy to that intention, too.

3. Tie your intentions and affirmations directly to your desire to deepen angel connections. If that's one of your main goals right now, then a perfect intention could be, "I will listen for the guidance my angels provide and work to communicate more with them every day." As for an affirmation to recite, something like, "I have guardian angels on my side, and our connection deepens all the time" is perfect.

4. Lastly, if you're stuck on what intention, affirmation, or mantra is best for you right now, ask your angels! They know you, your life, and your heart—so who better to give a nudge toward what your positive self-talk should sound like? Ask your angels directly, and keep an eye out for signs pointing you toward a facet of your life to focus on with your intention-setting and affirmations.

CHAPTER 10

INCORPORATING NEW TOOLS AND PRACTICES

By now, I'm sure it's not much of a surprise that many of the metaphysical and New Age practices people turn to are very interconnected and can benefit from being used in concert with one another. It's rare for someone who has developed relationships with angels to stop there when it comes to their spiritual growth and wellness journey. Most of us are called to a variety of practices and tools for connecting to the spiritual, growing in ourselves, and healing from challenges. This chapter introduces you to some great complementary tools and practices and gives you quick insights into how they can pair with your angel practice to deepen the benefits you get from both.

You may find yourself drawn to one, a few, or all of these tools and practices. Exploring the metaphysical and spiritual is all about truly letting yourself explore. So do just that! Try out what you're called to, dig deeper in your research, and find the perfect blend of practices that makes your life feel whole and fully realized.

CRYSTALS

This isn't the first time crystals are coming up in this book, so it's safe to assume they're a great (and popular) option. If you live in a large city, you're guaranteed to have a crystal or metaphysical shop around, but even if you don't, online shopping makes it easy to find crystals.

Here are some options for selecting the crystals that are best for you:

1. Do some research! Use the guide in chapter 3 of this book or some online digging to get a sense of some of the best crystals out there to suit your goals and needs. Then head to a shop with those in mind.

2. Shop intuitively. This is the perfect chance to practice your intuition skills. Walk slowly around a crystal shop, touching or hovering your hand over any stones you're considering. Be slow and careful; don't rush. Instead, pay attention to any signals in your body, sounds you hear, or intuitive guides indicating that one crystal is the right fit for you or that another isn't. Once you're confident about the stones your intuition is nudging you toward, make your purchase, and *then* feel free to research the meanings or purposes of those stones. You may be surprised at how perfectly you were guided toward the ones you need.

3. Talk to a staff member! At a shop, expert staff will be able to listen to any intentions you have for your crystal use and guide you toward stones that will benefit you.

4. Ask friends to send you a crystal that resonates. If you have metaphysically minded friends, ask them if they'd be willing to select a stone to send you—one they feel drawn toward when they think of you. In this way, you're relying on someone else's intuition. When you receive the gift, look into the stone and its purposes and see how well they align with your current needs.

Now, how can you incorporate those crystals into your angel work and other joy-boosting practices?

+ As mentioned earlier, you can include some relevant and beloved crystals on your altar, a space dedicated to communicating with angels or other divine beings and passed loved ones.

✦ Hold a crystal that connects to your intentions while you meditate, communicate with angels, or journal.

✦ If you find a stone that offers you a huge boost of connection to your guardian angel, don't hesitate to find a way to wear the crystal or have it near you often so you know you have a "signal booster" ready to use.

CHAKRA WORK

Again, the topic of chakras spans many books all by itself. This section is merely a basic primer on the topic, allowing you to decide whether chakra work is something you want to dig into more as part of your spiritual growth and wellness journey.

Chakras are the energy centers of our bodies, and each of us has seven chakras. In a perfect world, each chakra is aligned, unblocked, and working properly with the others. As a result of our life challenges, however, blocks can occur, and we may begin to struggle with one or more of our chakras, each of which is responsible for part of the body and mind.

Yogi Cameron writes in a *MindBodyGreen* article, "When all of our chakras are open, energy can run through them freely, and harmony exists between the physical body, mind, and spirit."[13] Obviously, this is the goal, right? When a chakra is blocked, there are a variety of ways to unblock it, including some of our tried-and-true methods, such as meditating and using mantras.

But which chakra is blocked or acting up?

---

13   Yogi Cameron, "A Beginner's Guide to the 7 Chakras and How to Unblock Them," *MindBodyGreen*, October 29, 2021.

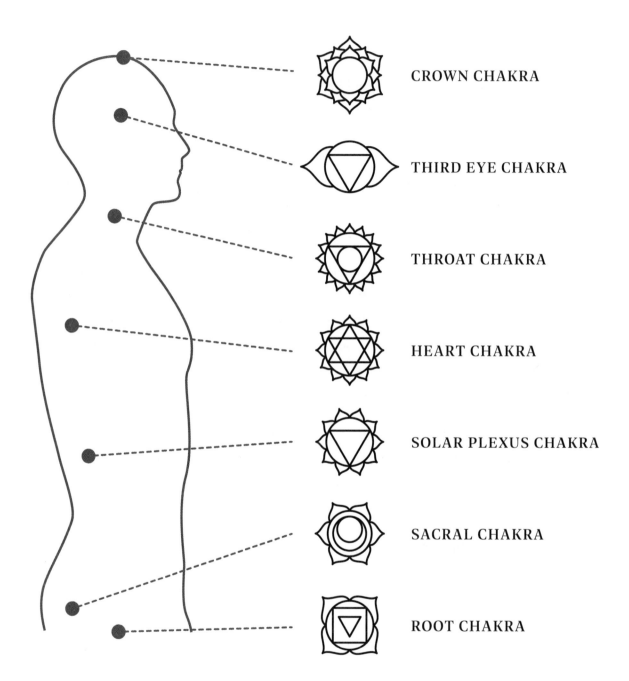

CROWN CHAKRA

THIRD EYE CHAKRA

THROAT CHAKRA

HEART CHAKRA

SOLAR PLEXUS CHAKRA

SACRAL CHAKRA

ROOT CHAKRA

THE ANGEL WORKBOOK

Root chakra: Located at the base of the spine, this chakra is key to your ability to feel grounded. Adds Yogi Cameron, "When the root chakra is open, we feel confident in our ability to withstand challenges and stand on our own two feet. When it's blocked, we feel threatened, as if we're standing on unstable ground."[14]

Sacral chakra: Based in the lower abdomen, this chakra rules emotional regulation, creativity, and sexuality. Challenges in those areas can definitely point to a block in the sacral chakra.

Solar plexus chakra: Further up in the abdomen, the solar plexus chakra rules your confidence. If you're feeling burdened by self-doubt and critical self-talk (if you're turning to affirmations all the time), you're probably struggling with a blocked solar plexus chakra.

Heart chakra: Bridging the gap between the lower three and upper three chakras, your heart chakra is a key component in the system, and its purpose is what you probably expect. This one is all about your ability to give and accept love freely, whether that means being loved by others, giving love to others, or loving yourself. Challenges in those arenas mean something's up with the heart chakra.

Throat chakra: In another highly logical relationship, your throat chakra guides you in using your voice and communicating your power and messages. Those struggling to express their feelings, speak up for themselves, or explain what they need should focus on this chakra.

Third eye chakra: Slowly connecting you more to your spiritual side, the third eye chakra is pivotal for your intuition, as well as your ability to see larger pictures and understand things below the surface. If you're getting tons of intuitive messages and signals, your third eye chakra is in great shape. If you're struggling to develop your intuition, start working on this chakra.

---

14   Yogi Cameron, "A Beginner's Guide To The 7 Chakras and How to Unblock Them."

Crown chakra: Situated right at the crown of the head, this chakra is your true gateway to the divine. It's very hard to fully open your crown chakra, and most of us don't, but this is the source of our spiritual power and ability to access higher consciousness.

How might chakra work tie into your angel work?

1. Working on opening your crown chakra is important in your development of spiritual awareness and your ability to engage with your higher consciousness, as well as beings such as angels.

2. Looking to improve your intuition so you're better able to sense those nudges and messages from angels? Time to unblock and open up that third eye chakra.

3. If you've been feeling overwhelmed by your own negative self-talk and poor self-image and affirmations and mantras aren't cutting it yet, it may be time to investigate blockages in the heart or solar plexus chakra that could be holding you back from true self love.

4. When you meditate in attempt to connect with angels, if you struggle with feeling grounded enough to become fully immersed in the meditation, take a deeper look at your root chakra.

Really, all the chakras go hand in hand. Your chakras are these incredible energy centers that have the power to help you be spiritually in tune, emotionally vulnerable, and fully open to love and kindness—all the things your angels also want for you. But if you struggle with blocks in some of your chakras, those goals are going to be harder and harder to achieve. So it's helpful to work in tandem on communicating with your angel and unblocking your stuck chakras. Opening up those chakras can offer you so much, not only when it comes to deepening your angelic connections, but also across all facets of your life.

PENDULUMS

Pendulums are fascinating, delightful tools used for an almost unlimited array of purposes. From seeking out water, to having your questions answered by divine beings, to learning more about yourself, a pendulum can offer you guidance on seemingly everything—including your angel practices. Once you have learned the programmed responses for your pendulum, you can use one to determine whether you have guides around, who they are, and how they can help you. This chapter's exercises include a basic exercise for setting up a pendulum and learning its responses so that you can try getting answers for these questions yourself.

ANGEL AND ORACLE CARDS

If you've long had an interest in angels, it's likely that angel cards have crossed your path at some point. Angel or oracle cards are decks similar in setup and often in appearance to tarot decks; they are just used differently. The decks are designed by artists who are also angelfolk (those who embrace angels and relationships with them), and they feature art that can range from images of specific or general angels to other spiritual imagery or divinely guided artwork. The decks also relay messages or wisdom—things your angels may be trying to convey to you right at this moment. Unlike tarot cards, there's no complicated methodology or system behind the decks, but simply messages directed to you via angels. So decks can be great to use as a tool to get your conversations going or to get a sense for who might be looking to communicate or the topic that might be concerning them.

Many who love oracle cards will encourage you to select and keep a few decks so you can choose the one you're feeling drawn toward on a particular day and have more variety in messages your angels can push your way.

Choosing and Using an Angel or Oracle Deck

Time to put this information to use. A deck to incorporate in your communications is a super easy option for your first tool, so I'd recommend getting one as a possible starting point.

PART ONE: CHOOSING THE RIGHT DECK

Just like selecting a crystal, the process of choosing one from the many hundreds of beautiful decks out there should circle right back to your intuition. Let your intuition lead the way. Not only is using your intuition easy and low-pressure, but it also allows your angels to nudge you, subconsciously, toward a great deck for you to use together.

1. Select a store to browse in with an array of decks to choose from. This may be a large mainstream bookstore, or better yet, an indie bookstore, a metaphysical shop, or the like.

2. Find the oracle and angel decks, and slowly look through all of them.

3. Consider these questions:

+ Do you find your gaze continuously returning to one in particular?

+ Did your body react to the sight of a particular deck on first glance?

+ Do any of them have unique images, markings, or titles that feel innately connected to you in some way?

4. When you find an option that seems to call out to you in one or all of these ways, it's likely you've deciphered where your intuition is pointing you. Try this deck and see what you make of it.

PART 2: USING YOUR DECK

1. For this process, have your angel journal on hand, as well as something to write with. Select a comfortable place to sit—perhaps at your altar, if you have one.

2. Open your deck and shuffle the cards, letting your intuition guide when you should stop shuffling.

3. Start simple: choose one card from the deck while it's facedown.

4. Look at the card you've chosen, and immediately take notes on the following prompts in your angel journal:

✦ What is your very first reaction to this card?

✦ What emotions does the image elicit? Joy, worry, confusion, excitement?

✦ How do you interpret the image on the card? Is it depicting a particular angel or some imagery or symbolism?

✦ What connection might this card have to your current life circumstances or the relationships you're developing with your angels?

5. If you choose, speak to your angels or the angel specifically pictured (if that's what's on the card), and ask if they have any meanings to offer surrounding this card pull. You may choose to leave it on your altar or somewhere else visible to guide your thoughts and communications for a few days.

6. In the future, when you feel comfortable, try choosing two or more cards at once, and see what messages you can glean from the combined cards.

Programming a Pendulum

Once you've selected your first pendulum, the next step is to get in tune with it and learn its responses so you can ask further questions and know what answer you're receiving.

I turn here to pendulum expert Richard Webster, who gives the perfect overview in his book *How to Use a Pendulum*:

> The easiest way to start using a pendulum is to sit down in front of a table with the chain of the pendulum held between the thumb and first finger of your dominant hand. . . . Rest your elbow on the table, and make sure that no other part of your body is in contact with it. Your legs should be uncrossed and your feet should be flat on the floor. The palm of the hand holding the pendulum should be face down, and the pendulum should hang seven to twelve inches in front of you.[15]

Once you've accomplished this positioning, here's your sequence of events:

1. Gently swing the pendulum, making both clockwise and counterclockwise circles in the air.

2. Change the swing pattern now, moving the pendulum from side to side and front to back.

3. Adjust your hold on the pendulum chain if it could be more comfortable so that you have the ideal holding position.

---

15   Richard Webster, *How to Use a Pendulum* (Woodbury, MN: Llewellyn, 2020), 13.

4. Then, still the pendulum's movement and ask your first question: "What movement will indicate a *yes* response?"

5. Wait patiently until the pendulum makes a movement that shows what its positive reply will be.

6. Once the pendulum is stilled again, ask, "What movement will indicate your *no* response?"

7. Again, wait quietly and patiently until the pendulum moves independently, showing what response will indicate no.

8. If your pendulum doesn't respond within a few minutes, try not to get discouraged. Just put it carefully away for the day and return to it to try again another time. Eventually it will respond to you, but working with a pendulum, like any new skill, can sometimes take a bit of time.

9. Aside from getting the pendulum's responses for yes and no, consider also asking for how it will move to indicate "I don't know" or "I can't answer."

10. Now, test the responses. As you might with a lie detector test, ask yes-no questions to which you know the definitive answer: "Is my name [*insert your name here*]?"; "Am I [*insert your age here*] years old?"; "Is it warm out today?"; and so on. Ensure that the answers the pendulum provides to these questions match the yes-no replies it showed you earlier, and you're ready to start asking more questions.

PUTTING IT ALL TOGETHER: ASKING FOR GUIDANCE

So now that you have a working pendulum, how can you use it? Well, you can ask any question you'd like confirmation about. For example, if you're considering a new mantra, what to manifest, which angel to communicate with, whether to take a new job offer— why not run it by your pendulum? Your angels may very well be the ones pushing that weight and giving the answer. You could also use the pendulum to start off your angel communication meditations or sessions. Ask, "Is [*insert the angel's name*] here now and ready to communicate?" When you get your answer, you'll know whether it's the right time to reach out.

ACTIVE EXERCISE

Unblocking Chakras

If you're struggling with blocks in one or more chakras that are keeping your body and soul from functioning in full, harmonious balance, there are plenty of ways to work to open the chakras back up. Some of the simplest include spending time in nature, reciting mantras, diffusing essential oils in your space, or detoxing from processed foods for a bit. But if you want to really maximize that unblocking, some other methods might also be worth a try.

YOGA MOVEMENTS FOR UNBLOCKING CHAKRAS

There are actually specific poses best for each chakra, so you can zero in on the spots that are causing you problems.

Warrior II   *Mountain*

For your root chakra, try a balancing pose. Common poses such as Mountain and Warrior require lots of steadiness and balance to achieve, which will help work out blocks in the root chakra.

Lotus   *Pigeon*   *Bridge*

For your sacral chakra, work on your pelvic floor. Poses such as Lotus, Pigeon, Bridge, and butterfly stretches will all help strengthen and open the pelvic floor, unblocking the sacral chakra.

Boat   *Side Plank*

For your solar plexus chakra, work your core. Based on the location of this chakra, core-strengthening poses such as Boat Pose, Side Plank, and Wheel Pose can all get you in better chakra shape.

Bow   *Cobra*

For your heart chakra, open your heart. Again, this should make sense—the location and power of this chakra means it's all about the heart. So, try Bow Pose, Camel Pose, Cow Face Pose, or anything else that opens up the chest, both literally and figuratively.

Plow

For your throat chakra, stretch the neck. Anything that naturally releases tension in your throat and neck is key here, so try Sphinx, Plow, or Fish Pose.

Downward Dog

For your third eye chakra, connect the separate parts of your body. It's essential here to find harmony and balance between your upper body and head and your lower body, putting you more in sync. Try a forward fold, Downward Dog, or Lotus Pose.

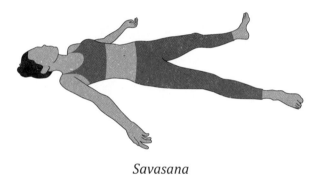

Savasana

For your crown chakra, finish your routine. Savasana (also called Corpse Pose) is a traditional ending to routines and a time for meditative reflection, relieving tension in the body, and breathing deeply. It's also the perfect pose to work out issues in your crown chakra, the space that connects you to higher consciousness. Savasana puts you in a great mind and body space to work toward that connection.

CHAPTER 11

HARNESSING SELF-EMPOWERMENT, AWARENESS, AND COMPASSION

We've worked through a lot of important topics and methods now, from reaching out to your guardian angels to angel journaling to following angel numbers. But before you head off on your own to deepen your angel relationships and invite their blessings into your life, I think it's important to cover some of the amazing ways your angels and their influence can help you grow, spiritually and emotionally. This growth is probably the most beautiful gift angels have to offer us, if we're just willing to accept it and use their guiding wisdom and love for our own benefit (and eventually for sharing with others).

There are some traits we almost universally seek out and hope to embody. We strive to be self-aware and independent. We want to be compassionate and genuinely caring. We want to feel joyful, peaceful, and content in life. We dream of feeling fulfilled and empowered in our lives. At times, these seem to be unreachable goals. Life has a harsh way of knocking us down more often than we are ready for. At other times, we may feel totally in tune with ourselves and our worlds, happily embodying these sought-after traits.

But it's in those harder moments, when summoning our empowered sense of self, radiating compassion, or reflecting with true self-awareness is truly a strain, that we can look to our angel guides for support and ultimately use their presence in our lives to grow and heal so we have fewer and fewer of those hard days and more of the beautiful, content ones.

FINDING YOUR HIGHEST POTENTIAL

Being the best we can be is the goal, right? Often seeming unattainable, this is what we may dream of when we meditate or despair for when we cry out for help. We want to reach our potential. We want to be our best selves.

Before we talk about self-improvement with the help of the angels, I think it's important to remind you of a few key things.

We should never strive for perfection. Aiming for perfection is setting ourselves up for endless disappointment. No matter how valiant our efforts, all people are imperfect. In fact, there is no suitable definition of a "perfect human." It is because of our flaws, our differences, and our uniqueness that we are who we are—that we are, after all, human. When we strive for more for our lives and ourselves, the goal isn't to achieve an illusion of perfection. The goal should be simply to *be good, do good, and feel good.*

Angels love you, no matter what. From the moment you were born, you had guardian angels on your side, watching out for you, rooting for you, and guiding you in subtle ways from the sidelines. These kind and loving beings don't exist to harm us, insult us, or tell us we aren't worthy of their love. We have it already. Rest easy knowing your angels will guide and support you no matter what mistakes you may make in this lifetime. Showing these angels your appreciation and love in return is the perfect response to the gifts they give.

HEALING YOUR EMOTIONAL CHALLENGES

When you're struggling and you know there's a solution, do you avoid requesting it, too embarrassed or proud to ask for help? More specifically, you communicate with angels and know they can help you work through emotional hardships, but are you still avoiding asking for their help? If you are, it's time to let down those walls. It doesn't make sense to have such a wonderful resource and not make use of it.

Life can hit us with a lot. Consider the emotional wounds and obstacles that may be holding you back from being truly happy, at peace, or free to share yourself with others. These might look like any of the following:

+ Unresolved wounds from childhood trauma
+ Triggers and fear instilled by trauma at any phase of life
+ Feelings of unworthiness or being unlovable
+ Fear of failure, rejection, or being alone
+ Lack of energy or enthusiasm about life
+ Challenges with vulnerability, trust, or opening up
+ Loss and grief
+ Ancestral wounds and patterns
+ Challenges to faith and spirituality
+ Anxiety and intense stress

This list is not comprehensive, and it's likely you've found yourself dealing with something else entirely, too. No one would ever say being alive is easy. However, working through these painful emotional hurdles and obstacles frees you to bring in more of the good, to experience more of the beauty of life. To find the joy and the life you're seeking, these obstacles and problems have to be worked through. You don't have to rush or push too hard. Ideally, you'll rely on support from friends, loved ones, or even therapists. But luckily, you also have some other teammates who can be huge supporters in leading you out of these painful emotional places. I think by now you know what supporters I'm talking about.

Consider focusing the efforts of your communications with angels on one or more of your emotional hurdles. Be direct—both with your angels and with yourself. Trust me, it will get you very far just to say something like "I know I need to work through my trauma in order to have the joyful, peaceful life I'm seeking; I would love your support and help on this path to a happier me." The more honest and direct you can be, the more your angels will be able to support you. It's hard to help someone who doesn't see the help when it's being offered—or refuses it outright.

Remember: There is no be-all and end-all that will cure problems such as trauma and mental illness. There may always be some elements of the struggle left in you. But if you work through the blocks the trauma has caused—pushing past the parts that keep you from moving forward and being happy—the hard and terrible things you may have been through will no longer have to define you. Instead, what you have endured can simply be part of what makes you unique, strong, and wholly yourself.

BECOMING WHO YOU WANT TO BE

Your angels and spirit guides wholeheartedly want you to be the happiest, best version of yourself. They are pushing for and guiding you to be all of these things:

+ Independent
+ Slow to anger
+ Confident and empowered
+ Successful
+ Compassionate
+ Self-aware
+ Peaceful and content

+ Happy and joyful
+ Kind toward all
+ Patient and understanding
+ Creative
+ Living your fulfilled, passion-driven life

If you need or want to work on some of these things, you know what to do, right? It's always as simple as asking your angels for support and help. You may find that becoming who you want to be takes time—big growth doesn't happen overnight. But if you make the personal effort and the right choices to embody the qualities you want to improve, all while conferring with your guides and asking for them to lead you in the right direction, rest assured you'll get there in time.

JOURNALING EXERCISE

Finding Your Purpose

Most of us aren't born knowing what we're meant to do with our lives. While some lucky few find their calling when they are young and stick with it, fully immersed in the passion and purpose of their lives, other people struggle to find what they're meant to do, ultimately spending a lot of time on pursuits that don't make them feel fulfilled and empowered. This pattern is normal. It's totally OK. And it's also time to do something about it. You get to enjoy one beautiful, glorious life in the body and consciousness you have now. Your one life is not worth wasting on things that don't make you feel alive, lit up, and totally psyched.

An important note: Even people who have found their life's purpose have bad days and days when they hate their jobs or feel burned-out. The difference is that they still feel intrinsically happy and at peace with what they're doing with their lives, rather than feeling that they're simply existing. You want to find that purpose and passion, but the goal isn't to live a perfect life every single day!

If you've struggled to find your purpose, take to journaling and reflect on the following prompts. Then follow the steps set out here to add your angels into the mix.

+ When you wake up in the morning, what can make you excited about the day, rather than bored or dreading it?

+ What activities, small or large, are guaranteed to put you in a good mood?

+ What activities or pursuits make you feel spiritually whole, as though you've reset your battery or filled your tank?

+ What activities drain you the fastest?

+ What are you naturally good at? Do you enjoy this feeling?

+ Without filtering or judging any of the ideas, assess all of your notes on these prompts, and list any professions, jobs, or pursuits that bring you more of what makes you happy to be alive and less of those things that burn you out.

Now, consider the list. You might have a wild range of ideas or a few solid options. It doesn't matter! This is a brainstorming phase. Now, reach out to your angel or guides in the way you prefer. Ask them directly. Say: "I'm trying to figure out my purpose in life and I would love your guidance. Please send a message or a sign if one of these ideas is right for me."

Be patient. Remember that sometimes messages take time to come in or for you to notice. Just focus on any potential clues, whether they take the form of an obvious response or a synchronicity that happens and points you directly toward an idea you had considered.

Building Qualities You Desire

Consider the qualities listed earlier under the heading "Becoming Who You Want to Be," ranging from being confident and empowered to being patient and understanding. It's time to do some self-reflection. Use whatever methods help you most, whether that means journaling, asking trusted loved ones (without becoming defensive), looking to the angels for wisdom, or even exploring your inner self in therapy. Hone in on some of the attributes that you think you may be lacking or need to deepen. We all have our flaws and weaker spots. Some of us might be incredibly empathetic and generous but lack the ability to care for ourselves or admit what we need. Others may be extremely confident about their own abilities but lack patience when it comes to the people around them. You may be incredibly creative and passionate but very hesitant to trust or communicate your feelings with others.

If you think you can parse out your own areas for improvement by yourself, great! If you have people in your life you'd trust to be honest with you about where you should focus your self-improvement efforts, ask them, and listen openly to what they have to say. When you know what you want to work on, try this short meditation-turned-angel-chat.

Sitting in a comfortable position, close your eyes and begin your process of deep breathing. Inhale deeply while you count to four, hold for a count of four, and then exhale through your mouth for another count of four. Repeat this process several times until you can feel your body relax and your thoughts slow.

Now focus your thoughts on yourself. More specifically, envision in your mind's eye the version of you that you're dreaming of: the one who is more confident, more self-aware, more patient, more compassionate—whatever the case may be. See yourself embodying these powerful traits. In your mind's eye, picture these qualities as physical entities, each a small, warm blip of light, entering your body gently through the top of your head. Picture yourself standing up as little spheres of light, each representing an important facet of yourself you want to work on, enter your body and slowly light you up more and more from the inside.

Picture your body becoming warmer and warmer, without ever becoming uncomfortable. Picture yourself feeling lighter, freer, more joyful and fulfilled. Let those sensations and feelings wrap around you and encircle you, like a warm, comforting hug.

Say to yourself: "I am capable of becoming the person I dream of being. I contain so much beauty and love, and I will channel these qualities as I go forward, embodying the things that are important to me."

Now, reach out to your angels. In this calm, happy state, call to any angels generally or to a specific guide or guardian who you feel will help you in your growth. Speak openly and honestly, remembering they know you intimately and are not there to judge you. Your angels have only the best intentions of loving you and guiding you toward this empowered version of yourself.

Tell them the things you're working on. Say: "I know that being my best self will take work on my end, too, but if you can help me along the way I will always appreciate it. Thank you."

Wait a moment to see whether you feel, hear, or sense a response, but know that even if you don't, your angel heard you and will be there every step of the way as you work toward the you you're dreaming of being and the life that will make you feel endlessly happy.

Once you feel satisfied with your conversation and your envisioning, take a few more slow, deep breaths as you come back to your body and open your eyes.

Now, moving forward in your day and life, pay attention to nudges from your angel around this growth journey. If you're working on patience and feel a push or a signal in a particular moment, slow down and assess: How can I embody more patience right now? Or if you're trying to love yourself more, watch for nudges from your angel—they'll come at the moments when you have a great chance to show yourself that love and care you deserve.

And remember, angels will help you in any ways they can. But being human is also about learning from mistakes and growing through challenges. You will have to tackle some hurdles, put in the effort, and perhaps stumble a bit at times in this journey to be the person you're dreaming of being. But you will get there, and you'll have your angelic team rooting for you and opening doors for your success the whole way.

CONCLUSION

You made it, my friend. I hope this journey opened your eyes and your heart to the warm, loving presences that exist in your life. I hope that you've found methods that align with your heart and soul and let you connect to angels anytime you need their wisdom, support, or sweet comforting love.

On some level, I think we all know we aren't alone in this world. And that's true in more than one way. We have people here on this plane who care for us, root for us, and want us around. But it can also bring great comfort to know that there are ever-kind and loving beings beyond our physical realm who also have our backs.

This book was designed to be a tool you use often—not something you run through in one sitting and never revisit. Please think of the book as a lifelong component of your spiritual journey, which you can write in, return to, reflect on, and share with others.

From here, I hope you dive even deeper. Ask your angels for more wisdom. Read more books. Watch videos, listen to meditations, explore new practices, find friends who share your spiritual interests. Question things until they become clear. Immerse yourself in whatever makes you feel whole and alive. Wherever your beautiful journey takes you, I wish you nothing less than a life of joy, love, and peace. And so do your angels.

APPENDIX

AN (ALMOST) COMPREHENSIVE LIST OF ANGEL SIGNS AND SIGNALS

Scattered throughout this book are various pieces of information about ways angels might reach out to leave a clue, a message, a signal that they're around and supporting you or hoping to communicate. This book is all about practical application, so for easy reference, it seems fitting to include a list of these possible signs all in one place. Wondering whether you might be getting nudges from an angel or what to look for? Consult this list; it will be a great guide for tracking those messages and signs throughout your life.

- ❑ Angel numbers, especially repetitions of the same cardinal number or the same sequence
- ❑ Feathers, especially white
- ❑ Gentle touch sensations, with no clear cause (as though someone has brushed your arm)
- ❑ Beams or bursts of light
- ❑ Shimmering, shifting, or unique light movements
- ❑ Full, embodied presences (humanlike or angelic in form)
- ❑ A beautiful scent passing by, without a clear source
- ❑ Faint, delicate sounds

- ❑ Flickering candlelight at key moments
- ❑ Voices, either audible or inside your head
- ❑ Whispers
- ❑ Mental images that pop up, especially if they do so repeatedly
- ❑ Synchronicities
- ❑ Messages via angel and oracle cards
- ❑ Significant dreams, or images or messages in dreams
- ❑ Persistent intuitive nudges
- ❑ Images in clouds
- ❑ Unusual weather patterns
- ❑ Animal appearances (such as the appearance before you of an animal considered sacred, loved by passed relatives, or unusual to the area)
- ❑ Getting some unexpected and particularly wise advice
- ❑ Hearing an important song in a significant moment
- ❑ A color, number, or the like that you consider lucky appearing often
- ❑ Images of angels showing up in your daily life
- ❑ Shapes like hearts appearing in unusual places
- ❑ One-time ringing in the ears
- ❑ Rainbows
- ❑ Chills
- ❑ A sense of not being alone, that someone is nearby
- ❑ Unexpected success and accomplishments
- ❑ Finding coins in unusual places
- ❑ Hearing something in the media around you at just the right time
- ❑ A flower in an unexpected place
- ❑ A warm feeling in the body

NOTES

REFERENCES

Carroll Richardson, Tanya. "10 Things You Probably Don't Know About Your Intuition." *Llewellyn*, November 26, 2018. https://www.llewellyn.com/journal/article/2722.

———. *Angel Intuition.* Woodbury, MN: Llewellyn Publications, 2018.

Cholle, Francis P. "What Is Intuition, and How Do We Use It?" *Psychology Today*, August 31, 2011. https://www.psychologytoday.com/us/blog/the-intuitive-compass/201108/what-is-intuition-and-how-do-we-use-it.

Handwerk, Brian. "Evolution of Angels: From Disembodied Minds to Winged Guardians." *National Geographic*, December 24, 2011.

Kerendian, Danielle. "Mantras vs. Affirmations: What's the Difference?" *Integrative Nutrition*, August 10, 2016. https://www.integrativenutrition.com/blog/2016/08/mantras-vs-affirmations-what-s-the-difference.

Mystic Michaela. *The Angel Numbers Book.* Avon, MA: Adams Media, 2021.

Valentine, Radleigh. *Compendium of Magical Things.* Carlsbad, CA: Hay House, 2018.

Webster, Richard. *Angels for Beginners.* Woodbury, MN: Llewellyn Publications, 2017.

———. *How to Use a Pendulum.* Woodbury, MN: Llewellyn Publications, 2020.

———. *Spirit Guides and Angel Guardians.* Woodbury, MN: Llewellyn Publications, 1998.

Yogi Cameron. "A Beginner's Guide to the 7 Chakras and How to Unblock Them." *MindBodyGreen*, October 29, 2021. https://www.mindbodygreen.com/0-91/The-7 -Chakras-for-Beginners.html.

ACKNOWLEDGMENTS

I appreciate so many people for so many things, but I'll keep this relatively brief. Thanks to Claire Sielaff for not only choosing to work with me on this project, but for guiding me through every step. And a huge shout-out to Cathy Cambron for truly excellent editing. Thanks, also, to the very talented team at Ulysses Press, who made this cool little book look so awesome and actually come to life. Thanks to all the authors I once worked with at Llewellyn, whose excellent ideas and writing informed me and sometimes even ended up quoted in these pages.

Thanks to all my parents for believing me when I said I was going to write books, and being impressed every time I do. And extra thanks to my mom for instilling such an aggressive love of reading that eventually I had to go write things myself. Huge and never-ending thanks to Shelby for being not only a fab cousin, but also my writing mentor and inspiration for many years, and for leading me toward so many opportunities I wouldn't have had otherwise. Thanks to the rest of my family, too, for being excited about the things I do.

Thanks to Grace, the kind of incredible friend everyone deserves, who somehow still wants to listen to me ramble on the phone anytime, every time.

And last, thank you to Jared, for believing in me so much that I do, too, and for being genuinely psyched about every seemingly small thing I accomplish, both in this project and in life. Your kick-ass support and love has made writing books way less daunting (and life better).

ABOUT THE AUTHOR

Annie Burdick is a Midwest native now based in Portland, Oregon. She worked previously as a New Age book editor before turning her focus to writing. This is her fifth nonfiction book. She spends most of her free time attempting to make a dent in her massive bookshelves, decorating her house with weird old treasures, and hanging out with her charming rescue dogs. She's probably drinking an iced tea and worrying over synonyms right now.

Find her online at AnnieBurdickFreelance.com.